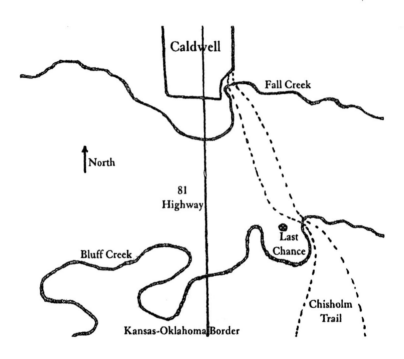

CALDWELL

Kansas Border
Cow Town

Tom S. Coke

HERITAGE BOOKS
2005

HERITAGE BOOKS

AN IMPRINT OF HERITAGE BOOKS, INC.

Books, CDs, and more—Worldwide

For our listing of thousands of titles see our website
at
www.HeritageBooks.com

Published 2005 by
HERITAGE BOOKS, INC.
Publishing Division
65 East Main Street
Westminster, Maryland 21157-5026

Copyright © 2005 Tom S. Coke

Other books by the author:
Old West Justice in Belle Plaine, Kansas

International Standard Book Number: 0-7884-3569-8

In Memory of

Richard L. Lane

A Great Historian

Contents

Acknowledgements

Many people have helped me research and write this book. Besides Kansas authors and editors and their outstanding works, such as Nyle Miller and Joseph Snell (*Why the West was Wild*), David Dary (*The Buffalo Book* and *Cowboy Culture*), Robert Richmond (*Kansas*), and Craig Miner (*Kansas* and *Wichita: The Early Years*), less known local historians I've met have contributed enormously to my knowledge of early Caldwell. Among those are Donald and Gloria White and Rod Cook.

Donald has spent many hours collecting local newspaper articles related to Caldwell. So far he has written and edited two collections in book form. The Whites have an impressive collection of photographs on historical Caldwell.

Rod Cook also has researched Caldwell's history for a number of years. His book on the Red Light Saloon included many details not generally known about southern Kansas cow town. His personal collection of books and maps related to historic Caldwell tells of his abiding interest and knowledge.

The Wellington, Kansas, public library provided many unique sources of reference material in addition to microfilmed newspaper articles telling about Caldwell's history. And so did the Sumner County Historical Society's collection found in Wellington's Memorial Auditorium next to the library.

A number of others, though remaining unnamed, have helped. I hope my poor memory doesn't make them think they haven't.

I would be remiss if I didn't mention my wife, Bobbi. She has always offered her help and encouragement in whatever writing project I have begun.

Caldwell Timeline

January 1871	Caldwell Town Company is formed.
July 3, 1871	George Peay is shot and killed.
February 1872	William Manning is shot and killed.
April 1, 1872	Mike McCarty kills Dan [Eugene] Fielder.
April 1872	Mike McCarty kills Doc Anderson.
April 11, 1872	Vigilantes kill Mike McCarty.
April 28, 1872	Vigilantes kill Jack Lynch.
June 1872	Caldwell posse chases horse thieves.
June 1872	Vigilantes kill Tom Ford.
July 1874	Drought, horse thieves, Indian scare plagues Caldwell.
July 4, 1874	Freighter Pat Hennessey is burned and killed.
July 30, 1874	Vigilantes lynch three horse thieves.
August 1, 1874	Grasshoppers plague Kansas.
Summer 1875	Local cattle business declines. People ask for a railroad.
March 1876	Chisholm Trail in Kansas closes.

Early 1877	Cherokee Strip opens to settlers.
May-July, 1877	Railroad proposals and elections fail.
September 1878	Railroad competition heats up.
July 1879	George Flatt kills two cowboys. Town incorporates.
August 7, 1879	Caldwell elects Mayor Noah J. Dixon and city officers.
August 1879	Mayor Dixon appoints George Flatt as first city marshal.
December 31, 1879	Special election decides on Santa Fe tracks to Caldwell.
April 12, 1880	Mayor Mike Meagher appoints Marshal William Horseman.
May 31, 1880	Cowley, Sumner, and Fort Worth Railroad reaches Caldwell.
June 13, 1880	First train arrives in Caldwell.
June 19, 1880	George Flatt is killed.
June 25, 1880	Sheriff arrests Caldwell mayor and police force for Flatt killing.
October 8, 1880	Former policeman Frank Hunt is killed at Red Light Saloon.
August 18, 1881	George Woods is killed at the Red Light Saloon.
November 1881	Merchants and Drovers Bank in Caldwell defaults.
December 17, 1881	Jim Talbot (Sherman) kills former mayor Mike Meagher.
June 22, 1882	Bean brothers kill Marshal George S. Brown.

December 2, 1882	Henry Newton Brown becomes marshal.
March 6-8, 1883	Cattlemen form Cherokee Strip Live Stock Association.
May 14, 1883	Marshal Brown kills Spotted Horse.
September 29, 1883	Marshal Brown guards $50,000 in silver for CSLSA.
December 14, 1883	Marshal Brown kills Newt Boyce.
March 26, 1884	Marshal Brown marries Alice Maude Levagood.
April 30, 1884	Brown, Wheeler, and two cowboys hold up Medicine Lodge bank.
May 1, 1884	Brown, Wheeler, and cowboys are lynched.
November 15, 1884	Marshal John Phillips fatally shoots Oscar Thomas.
December 7, 1885	Enos Blair is lynched.

Introduction

Quintessential Cow Town

Caldwell, Kansas
Saturday, November 8, 2003

This gray, blustery, sometimes misty afternoon had no power to dampen my spirits as Caldwell, Kansas history buff Rod Cook drove me around this once lively Kansas cow town. We had eaten lunch in Belle Plaine, where we both lived, before heading out to the Sumner County border town, where Cook grew up. This day proved to be one of the most memorable in my life.

On the way there we talked about some of Caldwell's history. Rod had plenty of information at his fingertips. His book, *George and Maggie and the Red Light Saloon*, had just been published the week before.

As we crossed the Union Pacific tracks (once the Rock Island) entering town from the east, Rod pointed out that the defunct Santa Fe tracks had run east of the Union Pacific's. We drove a block or so south along the east side of the UP and jogged back east where we crossed over the Santa Fe track bed. Rod explained that the Santa Fe had run to the southern border of Kansas at a point about a half-mile east of the UP.

We went south out of town so I could again see where the Last Chance Saloon once stood. That was my original purpose in contacting Rod Cook for the second time.

I had hoped for more specific information about the Last Chance and the Chisholm Trail when I emailed him. I anticipated Rod would return my email with some brief description of the saloon's

location. Instead, he suggested we have lunch and then go to
Caldwell so we could see it up close.

After showing me the old Santa Fe rail bed, he drove us south
out of town. We crossed Fall Creek, turned east on a dirt road, and
traveled about a quarter mile. We crossed over the UP tracks, then
turned south on an access road paralleling the UP toward Bluff
Creek.

Rod maneuvered his car slowly and carefully around the
potholes in this one-lane dirt road just as Don White, another
Caldwell historian, had done with me several months earlier. (Don
also proved to be a wealth of historical knowledge on Caldwell
when I visited him and his wife, Gloria, in town. His two books,
The Border Queen: A History of Early Day Caldwell, Kansas and
The Caldwell Post, "Kansas" Post: Jan. 1879 – Dec.1880, included
large collections of newspaper articles on early Caldwell.).

When we'd gone a couple hundred yards along the access road,
Rod stopped the car and we got out. We walked into the field to our
east. Trees lined the far side of the field going north and south. The
tree line curved to the east at its north end. This marked the flow of
Bluff Creek.

"Cattle on the Chisholm Trail crossed Bluff Creek where the
creek starts to bend toward the east," Rod explained, "though the
trees probably weren't there then."

As we shielded ourselves from the blustery cool wind of this fall
day standing near the center of the field, Rod said we were probably
standing near where the Last Chance had been. Just to the north of
us, the farmer who plowed this field marked with sticks the location
of two hand-dug wells. This kept him from falling in the holes.
The Last Chance needed water as well as whiskey.

After taking this in, we headed back to Caldwell. In town Rod
noticed his gas gage nearly on empty.

"I'd better fill up," he said, "where the Red Light Saloon once
stood." He went to the station at the northeast corner of Central and
Chisholm Street.

"I thought the saloon was further north," I said.

2

"Not according to county records," he answered. "They show this to be the spot where George and Maggie Woods put the Red Light."

We left the station and headed south down Chisholm Street. When we reached the end of Chisholm, Rod turned off the road to the left (east). We got out and walked to where the UP tracks cross Fall Creek. Below us stood part of a concrete dam in disrepair. On the east side of the tracks below the dam I saw a shallow rock bottom area with gently sloping banks. "That's where the Chisholm Trail crossed Fall Creek," Rod explained.

I could imagine the ruckus and dust stirred up as thousands of cattle crossed here. Anyone who lived on the south side of Caldwell anywhere near Chisholm Street in the early 1870s would have experienced plenty of noise. They would have heard thousands of bawling cattle as well as the jingling spurs, whistling, and yelling of cowboy herders.

Now I had a much better idea of where the Chisholm Trail entered Caldwell, where it crossed Bluff Creek, and where the Last Chance hung its shingle. But Rod Cook still had more to show: this time the southern end of the old Santa Fe Railroad where the cattle pens and loading chutes processed the herds during cattle drive days. We headed south again and continued to the Kansas-Oklahoma state line.

At the state line road we turned east. Rod looked for the Santa Fe rail bed that would be on the left side of the road. Spotting it proved to be a challenge, but not more than he could handle.

We parked at the side of the road and walked over to the barbed wire fence enclosing the field. He straddled the fence but had to help me between the wires. (In a basketball game he could have blocked my shots without leaving the floor).

"You can usually find railroad pikes or other evidence of the trains and cattle drives," he said. We walked north along the bed, looking for evidence, but I could find nothing. He eventually found two-and-a half inches of a round-headed ¾ inch diameter broken

3

rusty metal bolt with part of the threaded end (about seven threads) on it. He gave it to me.

"That probably came from a train," he said.

While searching for remnants, I had happened to notice something unusual. Throughout the crevices and craggy surface of the red earth next to the track bed sprouted a number of prickly pear cactus plants.

"Why all the cactus?" I asked.

"I can't help but believe that the Texas cows and horses carried the seeds intermingled in the hairs on their legs," he said.

This day filled my head with images of trail driving days. I had to agree with Bill O'Neal, who said about Caldwell, "In just the right light it is not difficult to imagine the sounds of a frontier saloon, of cattle hooves, of gunfire."[1]

A Town to Reckon With

Charlie Stone never lacked confidence. He'd made a name for himself in the cattle business before heading west and landing in Wichita, Kansas in 1869. There he became a leading merchant, running a tobacco shop. But he remained restless.

Word on the street said a better opportunity knocked at the door south of Wichita. Stone stormed the door. In 1871 he traveled to the southern border of Kansas and spotted some land overlooking Fall and Bluff Creek to his south next to Indian Territory. Soon he and his friends staked out some land and had it plotted. It stood on the Chisholm Trail.

Stone and friends named the place after a railroad magnate and Kansas politician they admired named Alexander Caldwell. Within a decade Caldwell became a thriving cattle town, fulfilling Stone's dream for it. For one season it shipped more cattle east than did Dodge City.

No one denied it had flaws. It saw more lawmen killed in its short cow town history than did any other. It also had all the business it could handle. And it saw its share of hardy pioneers not afraid to face any hardship that came.

In that short time between 1870 and 1885 it attained an enviable image, at least enviable to cowboys and easterners who read about it. Its reputation as a rip snorting pleasure spot for boisterous trail drivers at the end of the trail beat all competition.

Caldwell went from one crisis to another, from killings to lynchings, shootouts to search parties, bank openings to bank busts. Seldom was it boring. Often homesteaders and farmers wished it were.

Caldwell had trouble finding good lawmen to handle the lawless crowd that filled its many saloons. When it finally found an efficient lawman, he proved to be a little too efficient, that is, too good at killing.

The characters who walked the streets of Caldwell showed what a real cow town looked like. They provided a picture of the cow town both in its glory and in its shame. Yet in a way Caldwell became more than typical.

Of all the towns, it perhaps represented them better than any other for at least two reasons. First, it stood almost within shouting distance of Indian Territory and all its dangers. And second, it attracted cowboys over a longer period than any other. Abilene only had a couple of good cattle years before losing the trade. The same held for Wichita, Ellsworth, and Newton. Dodge City lasted a little longer, but cowboys didn't visit the place till the middle 70s after the buffalo business ended.

Since Caldwell stood next the Chisholm Trail, it had visits from cowboys from its earliest days in 1871 till its closing days in 1884 and 1885. True, the early days saw trail drivers stopping for supplies and occasional drinks before heading further north. But this became a thriving seasonal business. Then when the Atchison, Topeka, and Santa Fe railroad built to the town in 1880 the place boomed even more.

Through these years it experienced Indian scares and fights, cattle thieves and killers, lawmen chasing outlaws, lynchings, financial schemes, and continuing conflict among cattlemen, trail herders, merchants, farmers, and homesteaders. Its location next to the Cherokee Outlet to the south sustained it in the lean years after Texas herds and before the railroad. The Cherokee Strip Live Stock Association, made up of wealthy cattlemen located in the Cherokee Outlet, provided steady business as its cattlemen traded and sometimes lived in town.

From all these groups living, dying, fighting, growing, prospering, and struggling for success came a number of true and fascinating accounts, many unknown to most people, including Western lore lovers. These events make up the story of Caldwell. They make up a brief though interesting piece of American history.

◊

Throughout its years as a cow town, Caldwell had competing groups of citizens. The three main ones, cattlemen, trail drivers, and farmers, had competing agendas. A fourth group, merchants, welcomed business from all.

Trail drivers wanted open range so they could move and graze cattle before selling them. Cattlemen wanted closed rangeland to grow their domesticated herds for market. Farmers wanted a protected area to work their soil, plant and raise their crops. So each group bumped heads with the others.

First came cattle herds from Texas to railroads in Kansas along the Chisholm Trail. (Actually Baxter Springs in southeastern Kansas saw the first herds shortly after the Civil War along the Shawnee Trail. But that didn't last long.) As the herds shifted their business from Abilene to Ellsworth, Newton, and Wichita because of developing railroad lines, Charlie Stone and others saw the continuing flow of traffic along the Chisholm Trail and tapped in to it.

At first, business in Caldwell centered on bypassing cowboys. Stone staked his future on this transient business. But merchants knew a railroad to Caldwell would expand this booming business even further. So it worked toward that end.

Railroads actually played key roles in developing Caldwell and the entire state of Kansas before the cattle trade. President Abraham Lincoln signed the Homestead Act during the Civil War but settlers didn't pour into the Western lands until railroads did their job of advertising.

"Both natives and foreigners who peopled the Great Plains were attracted by the most effective advertising campaign ever to influence world migration," said Ray Allen Billington. "Steamship companies, anxious to reap a harvest of passenger fares, invested heavily in European newspaper space, marred the walls of half the Continent with their posters, and provided free transportation for immigrants wishing to revisit the old country providing they urged others to return [to America]. Western states maintained immigration bureaus in the East and Europe, where hired agents scattered propaganda and urged farmers to migrate to the land of plenty . . .

"Their efforts were surpassed by those of the West's principal colonizers – the land-grant railroads. They stood to benefit doubly from western settlement; newcomers would not only buy their land but create way traffic previously lacking in the sparsely settled region."[2]

So homesteaders began to populate southern Kansas before cattle drives came into their own. But once trail drives began along the Chisholm Trail, entrepreneurs with an eye on ways to make money saw these traveling cowboys and cattlemen as a real market. And Charlie Stone became a leading entrepreneur for this market. But most didn't realize how short-lived the trail driving traffic would be.

While trail driving increased, so did pioneering settlers. These homesteaders continued to fill Kansas country, plowing the sod on their quarter sections and planting seed for their crops. This couldn't help but conflict with trail drivers and cattlemen who hoped to run cattle on open range.

Cattlemen found one answer to their problem when they grazed their cattle in the Cherokee Outlet south of Caldwell. But this aggravated the animosity between farmers and ranchers since the U.S. government banned homesteaders from the Outlet. When settlers tried to stake their claim there, government troops kicked them out. Yet cattlemen worked out deals with Indian tribes to graze their cattle there.

While this conflict continued, Caldwell merchants profited from both businesses. Farmers and cattlemen spent money on goods and services in town. Of course cowboys also spent freely on their vices, whether alcohol, cards, or women. So Caldwell profited and attracted increasing traffic. When 1879 business blossomed into a boom, it left the town with the title of Border Queen for good reason.

To understand Caldwell's early history, it's probably best to break it into two periods: early frontier years from 1870 through 1879; and the railhead years from 1880 to 1885. The town appeared quite different in these two times.

Before 1879 it never attracted more than several hundred people. But once people knew railroad tracks would reach the town, the place grew to a couple thousand.

The early years saw no city government. Caldwell depended on county and township officers to control lawlessness. Legal transactions took place at the county court at Wellington or district court in Wichita. Homesteaders and merchants mostly had to deal with local problems on their own.

The later railhead town incorporated and became organized under a mayor, city council, and city government, with a town marshal and deputies serving as the legal guardians. City ordinances spelled out the law and gave the town another way to raise money when lawbreakers were fined. But the town, like other Kansas cow towns, continued to suffer from rowdy cowboys even more after incorporating.

Early Caldwell reflected the characters who lived there. Some were outstanding businessmen. Others were tireless homesteaders and farmers who fought natural disasters and dangers daily without much notice. Some were natural leaders who led boldly. Others drifted to the wrong side of the law and often paid for it.

Sometimes Caldwell citizens organized only long enough to chase down their enemies and deal with them permanently. Their use of lynch law may look harsh by today's standards. But a close look at what they faced throws a different light on their behavior.

Border towns such as Caldwell could expect more trouble than towns further north or east during these early years in Kansas. Indian Territory lay two miles south. That served as welcome refuge to any criminal on the run. So horse thieves and murderers found it to be the perfect escape route.

And once in Indian Territory, the outlaw could hide nearly anywhere. Few lawmen risked even riding through that area. If a settler didn't know better, he would ride into the Territory straight into an outlaw gang, or if lucky enough to avoid that, into an Indian band wanting revenge for mistreatment by the U.S. government. Any way you look at it, his chances for survival dropped going south.

Not until 1875 did Judge Isaac Parker assign deputy marshals to oversee that area. So any homesteader who lived near there, and some of the earliest one around Caldwell did, had to be from hardy stock to survive. In fact, a number of early settlers around Caldwell located near Fall or Bluff Creek only a stone's throw from the Territory. That's the kind of people Caldwell started with.

During this time, Caldwell felt danger from all sides. Cowboys roamed the streets and saloons while resting up from cattle drives. Some stirred up trouble while hardy pioneers bought supplies, met with friends to talk crops, and shared the latest news and rumors.

Entrepreneurs welcomed all business. Lawmen kept an eye on suspicious characters. Outlaws gave lawmen reason to be suspicious.

In Caldwell, ordinary and not so ordinary people faced numerous challenges in this growing cow town. This town reflected a piece of American history that developed into legend. Gunfighters and gunfights took place, but perhaps not quite in the way the Western later told it. The true account of what happened, though, might prove to be just as interesting as the tales that spread in the following century.

1

"Uncle Sam, at that time, had plenty of land."

Charles H. Stone possessed extraordinary qualities typical of 19th century Americans who ventured west. He perpetually sought ever-new avenues to success. By 1870 Stone knew where his best chance of success resided. It had to do with an Illinoisan named Joseph McCoy. And it had to do with Stone's experience since age 21.

Though Massachusetts was Charles Stone's birthplace in 1841, what he learned at an early age about cattle propelled him westward. He grew up more of a country boy than a city slicker.

By the time he finished high school he was ready to head west for open land. He landed in Peoria, Illinois for a year, moved to Lawn Ridge where he worked in the cattle business for three years, and with this experience moved further west to Missouri and then Topeka, Kansas.[3]

This was around the time McCoy was showing others the new way to make money. All you had to do was trail cattle north from Texas to the Abilene, Kansas railhead town where cattlemen could sell their stock at double and triple their price. While this downplayed the hardships, by 1870 McCoy showed it could be done profitably.

Charles Stone didn't need much push to develop his interest in this business. So even the earliest signs of profits whetted his appetite. Stone paid attention to other enterprising people in Topeka who were open to the business possibilities of this burgeoning trade.

In the spring of 1868 a group of Topeka men formed the Wichita Town Company. They wanted to legally incorporate a town site at the fork of the Arkansas Rivers. They failed at that time but did decide on the name of Wichita. They also sent Darius Munger to the area to check it out.[4] Munger's reports to the Topeka group encouraged others to settle there. Hearing about this convinced Charles Stone to take the plunge. He headed to Wichita and opened a business selling tobacco for about a year. He then got back in the cattle business.

Charles Stone's ever-active business mind saw greater opportunities along the Chisholm Trail further south. For the next four years after 1867, cattle drives grew in number. He figured there would be less competition for a larger share of profits at an undeveloped though well located spot along that route.

It didn't take Stone long to figure where the least competitive place with the best opportunity for business success would be - where the trail entered Kansas. He figured out several reasons for that.

After traveling north through Indian Territory where alcohol was prohibited, what better place for cowboys and cattlemen to stop for refreshments than at the Kansas border? It would be an excellent place to provide supplies to herders who still had a ways to go before Abilene.

But Stone saw an even greater reason for success. Just south of Caldwell lay acres of fertile grassland. Cattle could graze and fatten up there before heading further north. Or cattlemen could stick around till they found buyers around Caldwell.

And even more important, quarantine lines had no effect on them. Keep in mind, Kansas law even before the Civil War outlawed all Texas cattle from entering the state. Settlers in the 1850s knew Texas cattle brought disease.

On December 13, 1855, Missouri outlawed Texas cattle after suffering from such herds. When Texans headed to Baxter Springs, Kansans experienced the same. On February 1, 1859, Kansas Territory passed a law to outlaw any cattle entering from Texas, Arkansas, or Indian Territory between June 1 and November 1. On May 1, 1861, the new state of Kansas passed the same type of law.[5]

This didn't stop Texas trail drivers from illegally doing business during the Civil War. But it did give Kansans a legal basis for penalizing them when they were caught.

After the war, the situation changed. Veterans returning to Texas found hundreds of thousands of wild longhorn cattle roaming the countryside after a half decade of neglect. The eastern market begged from beef.

The Kansas legislature decided they needed to modify the 1861 law. On February 26, 1867 they added an exception. The new law prohibited Texas cattle between March 1 and December 1 but allowed it west of the sixth principal meridian. "This area was bounded by a line from the southern boundary of Kansas northward to about sixteen miles east of McPherson, and then turned west to the Colorado border," said William Zornow.[6]

This still left Wichita, Newton, Abilene, and later Caldwell within the quarantined area. Joseph McCoy knew how to fudge a bit and got Governor Samuel Crawford to go along with him. But Charles Stone didn't want to be forced to depend on the governor's largesse.

Near the end of 1870 Stone and fellow Wichita businessman James H. Dagnar, a liquor wholesaler, headed south to check out the Chisholm Trail at the Kansas border. They found a spot overlooking the two creeks to the south (Fall and Bluff). This was about as close as you could get to Indian Territory at the time, since the Cherokee Strip area was still in dispute.

Except for one man, John E. Reid, who settled on the banks of Fall Creek on October 14, 1870, the area was uninhabited.[7] Stone and Dagnar didn't hesitate. They hurried back to Wichita with dollar signs flashing before their eyes.

Stone and Dagnar shared their ideas with several others in Wichita. This included Charles Gilbert, G.A. Smith, George Vantilberg, and Chris Pierce. Stone returned to the border area with a survey party in January 1871 and staked out the future town.

The Wichita group formed a town company, purchased 113 acres on Fall Creek, and named the border town Caldwell.[8] Gilbert served as the company's president, Smith as secretary, and Stone as treasurer.[9] The name the group gave the town reflected views of the town company members.

The town's namesake, Alexander T. Caldwell, born March 1, 1830 in Huntingdon County, Pennsylvania, grew up fast. In his teens he clerked in a Columbia, Pennsylvania store till his father, James, joined the army in 1847 to fight in the Mexican War. Alexander, then 17, quit work to join up in his father's company.

His father died that September at the battle of Chapultepec. Alexander fought in several more battles before the war ended and then sought his fortune on his own.

He learned about banking by working as a cashier at the First National Bank of Columbia, Pennsylvania. He moved to Leavenworth, Kansas in 1861. There he started A. Caldwell & Company, which hauled army supplies to military posts. At one time he employed 5,000 men.

He worked in railroad construction. He contracted to build the Missouri Pacific Rail Road from Kansas City to Leavenworth in 1866 and extended the line to Atchison. He and others organized the Kansas Central Rail Road Company and built it from Leavenworth to Miltonville, Kansas.

By this time he was admired as a leading Kansas citizen. In 1871 he became a United States senator.

He knew how to make money and use money to make more money. Maybe he knew it too well. But this caught Charlie Stone's eye. Stone admired Caldwell for the same reasons Stone sought more fortunes further southwest in Kansas. Caldwell knew how to succeed in business.

Stone and the other Caldwell Town Company leaders saw that name as the epitome of what they stood for. Even when Alexander quit the Senate two years after his election under questionable circumstances, the town company members stuck with the name, believing the accusations against Caldwell were simply a political game played by Democrats.[10]

Charlie Stone wasted no time in getting down to business. In late February 1871 he hired a crew to cut down hackberry and cottonwood trees and construct a building for the first business in Caldwell. He and Dagnar opened a "grocery store with liquid groceries preponderating."[11]

They opened the store in time for the 1871 cattle drives headed for Abilene and Wichita. That year, the busiest in history, saw more than a half million cattle headed north from Texas

Stone anticipated a good turnover from the cowboys and cattlemen stopping at Caldwell long enough to quench their thirst, buy some supplies, eat some grub, maybe get some rest – a break from the monotonous and strenuous job of keeping cattle moving in the right direction.

He was not disappointed. In fact, he must have been surprised, if not shocked, by how much business he got from the start. He took in $711 the first day.[12]

Other businesses followed. Milam Fitzgerald put up a 14 by 16 foot building and sold supplies. It also offered alcohol to thirsty cowboys. Several other characters were connected with this business, including "Jones and Heitrich, J.L. ['Deacon'] Jones, D.P. [Dave] Terrill and Hank Zuber.[13]

James M. Thomas put up a drovers' supply store, a 24 by 30 foot log building, and leased it to Cox and Epperson. Cattlemen and cowboys stopped there on their way to Abilene and Wichita.

Last Chance

A fourth store south of town may have been open around this time, though no records mention it till 1872. This was the most famous place near Caldwell in the town's early years, the Last Chance/First Chance Saloon. Cowboys and cattlemen on these drives ran into the Last Chance first since it was south of Caldwell, though they probably frequented it more on their way south after the cattle drives.

15

John E. "Curly" Marshall, the first person connected with this saloon and trader ranch, probably was the one who built the log house that contained supplies for trail drivers passing by. Marshall later built a frame structure next to the log house hoping to use it for a dance hall. He planned on hiring Wichita prostitutes to liven the business.

Curly Marshall was a big burly six-foot, 250-pound frontiersman who had served as a government scout with Company L, Second Missouri Cavalry during the Civil War. He later served as an Indian scout at Fort Harker.[14]

The Last Chance was located about one mile south of Caldwell nearly surrounded by Bluff Creek. The saloon stood at the center of a loop in the creek (creating something like a peninsula) with an opening to the north. George Freeman, an eyewitness in 1872, described it, saying "about 200 yards from the ranch is a ravine, running in a southeast direction and finally terminating in Bluff Creek. This creek in its winding course almost makes an island here, and the ranch is situated near the center of the ground in this enclosure."[15]

Curly Marshall may have picked this site because of its seclusion as well as access to regular traffic. He could buy supplies in Wichita or later Caldwell but could have his privacy of being out in the country, and he could depend on regular Chisholm Trail business at least during most of the year. This remote area worked out for him since he had a number of friends who lived on the wild side.

Curly Marshall's reputation preceded him. Before running the Last Chance, he had connections with a trader ranch on the Ninnescah River south of Wichita. It was known for the questionable characters that frequented it. By 1872 Caldwell settlers wished the Last Chance didn't exist. It offered stiff competition to Caldwell businesses. Besides that, Caldwell saw it as a center for a horse thief ring.

Horse theft by then was a real problem. And some of the main suspects were the most frequent visitors of the Last Chance.

"Uncle Sam, at that time, had plenty of land."

Between 1872 and 1874 many saw this as the biggest problem in
and around Caldwell.

◊

The first Caldwell pioneers came at the right time. That year,
(1871) was the busiest of all, as previously mentioned. An
estimated 600,000 head of cattle accompanied by 3,000 thirsty
cowboys made the journey north. And all those traveling on the
Chisholm Trail trampled by the new town of Caldwell.

The missing ingredient in these early years was a railroad. It
could provide a shipping point for cattlemen wanting to sell their
herd in Caldwell and having them hauled east to an open market.
But Charles Stone and his fellow businessmen held out that hope
and meantime made a profit from traveling cowboys.

In the early years of Caldwell, the town drew settlers with
different agendas. Farm families hoped to prosper with abundant
crops. They didn't care for the transient cowboys. Texas longhorns
had a way of trampling crops. Cowboys brought recklessness and a
way of life farmers feared would influence their children in the
wrong way.

On the other hand, businessmen saw profits from the trail drives.
After all, the drives brought untold numbers of customers. Certain
businesses, such as saloons, almost entirely depended on trail
driving cowboys.

Contrasting personalities showed up from Caldwell's beginning.
John Reid, who had already settled in the area before Charles Stone
arrived, provided an example of the early settler. Reid, born in
Scotland, moved to Illinois when still a boy. He learned farming
from his father. They moved to Missouri, where John farmed
before migrating west to the Caldwell area. By then he had a wife
and five children. Soon after arriving, his horse died, his family got
sick, his wife died, and he did everything in his power to support the
children. His experience was not uncommon to settlers.

George Freeman was another example. He may have been attracted to the Caldwell area in 1871 because of notices in Kansas papers asking for a blacksmith.[16] He said he came because of news about Sumner County being wide open for settlers.

"I, at that time, had a wife and three children," he said. "We all stood greatly in need of a home to call our own. Uncle Sam, at that time, had plenty of land around Caldwell, out of which to make homes for the homeless. I thought that the transient trade, afforded by the travel over the trail by Texas men with herds from Texas, could not fail to make a red hot town."[17]

Though he thought he could handle the hardships, he was surprised by just how difficult life could be. "Having lived in a civilized portion of Kansas for a number of years, I considered myself able and competent to battle with the roughs and privations of an early pioneer settler," he said. "But little did I dream of the insurmountable hardships of a frontier settlement."[18]

Freeman became the town's first blacksmith. He was also surprised by how easily unscrupulous frontiersmen could break the law, stealing horses, intimidating neighbors, fighting and killing others in gunfights. By April 1872 he became a township constable and lived to tell of many exciting experiences chasing outlaws and fighting gun battles.

Though Caldwell started as a rough and tumble supply center like other trader ranches along the Chisholm Trail, many local citizens held strong religious views. These views affected their behavior toward transient cowboys and businessmen in town.

One man not afraid to talk about his faith was the town's first doctor, B.W. Fox. He acted as a minister and helped others who preached in early Caldwell. On August 23, 1872, he performed the first wedding in town when George Grant married Christina Reid.[19]

Before the Presbyterian church in town began, Rev. Jacob B. Rideout, who had a claim about eight or ten miles east of town (around the Hunnewell area), traveled to Caldwell to preach. Sometimes it became too late for him to return home. He could not yet afford a horse. So he stayed with Dr. Fox. Rideout's wife remembered those times.

"My husband, after walking from eight to 16 miles and preaching three times during the Sabbath, would be too tired to walk home," she said, "and under such circumstances he would sleep in the doctor's office, on the floor, using a large book for a pillow."[20]

Most settlers, though, spent most of their time trying to survive rather than going to religious or political meetings. Danger came from a number of directions.

Disease killed many before they had a chance to prosper. Hostile Indians paid frequent visits. And the more settlers moved west, the more Indians saw their way of life threatened and fought for their own survival.

Transient trail drivers presented another danger. They like to celebrate. They visited saloons, got drunk, got into fights, and shot off their weapons.

If all that wasn't enough, everyday existence presented a huge challenge. Crops failed if there was not enough rain, too much rain, or cattle stamped through them. Prairie fires burned everything in sight. Outlaws, whether horse thieves or killers, roamed freely. No organized police force yet existed.

Vigilantes On the Rampage

Indian threats were constant from the time Caldwell began. A man known as Dutch Fred Crats, who lived on Bluff Creek near Reid's place at Fall Creek, ran headlong into trouble on June 15, 1871. Crats was headed home after shopping at Caldwell that Thursday morning. That day two Indians rode up to him about 1½ miles from town.

Crats rode a large mule. The Indians were on ponies. The Indians' greeting left Crats uneasy. One of them rode close to Crats and raised Crats' coat, checking for firearms. Crats knew he was in trouble. He had no firearms on him.

One Indian grabbed the mule's bridle. The other rode behind. They told Crats they were headed for a buffalo hunt.

Crats knew he had to escape or die. When the three neared a bend in Bluff Creek, Crats jumped off his mule and ran toward the brush.

One Indian fired at him. The Indian may not have had much experience with firearms. Likely he skimped on the powder, because the ball bounced off Crat's back. The other Indian shot an arrow. It pierced Crats' arm and tore into his shoulder. Crats jumped down a bluff and crossed to the south side of the creek.

The Indians knew their ponies couldn't navigate the steep bluffs so they circled around, looking for another place to cross. They took their time since they knew Crats was on foot and injured. But Crats had other plans.

He re-crossed to the north side and hid in some driftwood. He waited several hours.

His maneuver worked. Crats, losing blood rapidly, struggled back to John Reid's dugout. Reid fetched a doctor. Crats lived to tell his story, but was permanently disabled.[21]

◊

That spring and summer cattle drives through Caldwell reached their peak. Hundreds of thousands of head, usually with 15 or 20 cowboys driving herds numbering 1,500 to 2,500 continued north on the Chisholm Trail headed for Abilene. That year one of the cowboys driving cattle was John Wesley Hardin. His experiences along the trail showed what kind of characters took part in these massive drives.

Hardin was running from the law when he decided to go on a cattle drive with his cousins, the Clements brothers. Hardin and Jim Clements drove 1,200 cattle and Jim's brothers, Manning, Joe, and Gyp, followed with another herd. They left Texas in March.

"The day we crossed Red River, about fifteen herds had crossed," Hardin said. Cowboys tried to stay together through Indian Territory for protection from marauding bands. For that reason, and because of the large number of cattle drives that year, Hardin said the trail was one line of cattle with no one out of sight of another herd throughout the trip through the territory.[22]

On the way, Hardin got in several fights and killed several Mexican herders before passing by Caldwell on the way to Abilene. In Abilene, he shot a man and fled to hide out. While hiding out, he heard that Juan Bideno, a Mexican cowboy, had shot and killed cowboy Billy Cohron on Wednesday, July 5th. Hardin knew Cohron as a fellow Texan and trail driver. So Hardin decided to track the killer down. He heard from others in cow camps on the Chisholm Trail about Bideno's whereabouts and followed this information. He took along Cohron's brother and two others to help. He tracked Bideno to a restaurant and bar in Sumner City, a few miles north of Caldwell, where he ended up shooting and killing the man.[23]

Shoot and Run

Cowboys sometimes brought trouble. But so did residents. With little restraint from local law, more aggressive and less moral characters could flaunt their power. They could commit crimes and escape to the south. This lack of law combined with wild characters sometimes led to lead poison deaths.

On Monday, July 3rd, 1871, two men in Caldwell had it out. That day George Peay, who lived several miles east of Caldwell near Bluff Creek, and O. Bannon (or O'Bannan), who lived several miles west of town, were both in Caldwell.

Peay, a six-foot 200-pound troublemaker, was considered an obnoxious bully when drunk. Bannon, a small man who had come to Kansas from Canada, had the opposite reputation. He lived in a dugout with two other settlers, George Mack and H.H. Davidson. Mack became a justice of the peace in September. Davidson became a successful cattleman by 1873.

All day Peay had been drinking. Hoping to stop any trouble, some of his friends took Peay's gun from him. That didn't stop him. He continued to threaten others.

When Peay crossed paths with Bannon, Peay tried to pick a fight. Bannon declined. Peay followed Bannon, egging him on. When Peay made threatening moves toward Bannon, Bannon drew a cap and ball revolver and pulled the trigger. It misfired. "Count yourself lucky," Bannon told Peay. Next time could have different results.

They parted. Bannon borrowed a friend's gun in case the two met again. Later that day they did. Peay wanted to fight. This time Bannon drew the friend's gun, aimed, and fired. Peay fell back on the ground.

"God, boys, I'm shot!" Peay said. He soon died.

Bannon turned to some of Peay's friends. "If there's anyone here wants to take it up, they have the privilege of doing so," he said, "for I'm in good shooting order."

A few days later Bannon left town. He probably feared Peay's friends, who could be their own law, as much as any local law.[24]

The Peay killing forced Caldwell residents to deal with a growing problem. The town had no law. The closest police force was the Cowley county sheriff's office east of Sumner County. The only other form of police might be a deputy U.S. marshal passing through town.

Local residents looked to themselves for help. They formed a vigilante committee to deal with lawbreakers. Though the majority of the people were peaceful, law-abiding citizens, some weren't. Until the county, townships, and town of Caldwell voted for leaders, including a police force, vigilantes became the preferred alternative.

◊

While vigilantes organized in self-defense, other citizens pushed for a special election to choose county and local leaders. People voted on September 26, 1871. The closest precinct to Caldwell was A.M. Colson and J.A. Ryland's ranch six miles northeast. J.J. Ferguson, from Belle Plaine, became the first Sumner county sheriff. C.P. Epps and John J. Youell became constables in the fourth precinct, which included Caldwell.

Since the county seat was up for grabs, voter fraud appeared throughout the county. It seemed every town in the running accused other towns of cheating. For example, the *Oxford Times* published a parody of "The Battle Cry of Freedom" against rival Belle Plaine, accusing them of multiple votes from the same person.[25]

This early election left the county disorganized. It had little effect on lawlessness. Vigilantes still believed they had to take up the slack. On Tuesday, November 7, the county held a regular election. This time Caldwell served as one the voting precincts.

Caldwell experienced lax voting procedures, as did other Sumner county towns. According to George D. Freeman, who then lived in Caldwell, the November 7 election displayed a rampant free-for-all.

"The usual festivities of drinking whiskey, horse racing, and target shooting was indulged in by the cowboys," Freeman said. "The silence would sometimes be broken by some one throwing an old oyster can into the air, when some one would fire at it in rapid succession to ascertain how many balls he could put into it before the can fell to the ground."[26]

Another Killing

In February 1872 a man named Epps (perhaps Constable C.P. Epps) and William Manning, both living near Bluff Creek south of Caldwell, argued over a stack of hay. Manning and his brothers from Texas were holding cattle to be sold later.

Freeman witnessed some of the fight. He happened to be in that area that day. He talked to Epps about a missing horse. After leaving Epps, Freeman crossed paths with Manning who was headed towards Epps' dugout. Manning appeared disturbed.

Freeman continued on his way home. Shortly after that Freeman heard gunfire. He turned around and rode back to Epps' dugout.

Epps stood in the doorway and Manning lay dead outside. They had argued and Epps ended up shooting Manning. When Manning's brothers found out, they threatened to kill Epps. People who knew the Mannings said the brothers buried William a couple miles south of Caldwell at a place that became known as Manning's Peak or Lookout Mountain.

Epps went to Wellington and got a warrant for the Manning brothers' arrest for threatening him. The sheriff and two deputies chased the brothers, caught them, then took them to Caldwell. From there, the sheriff and his assistants headed back to Wellington with the prisoners.

About eight miles on their way north, they stopped at a ranch for a break. The guards played cards and drank while the Mannings were in their custody. The guards in fact became so distracted in their card game that the prisoners escaped and were never seen again in that area.[27]

25

Wanted: Mike McCarty

Less than two months later, in April 1872, Caldwell saw more bloodshed. How three men met their end that month would remain the talk of the town.

Since winter 1871-1872, Michael J. McCarty and Dan (or Eugene) Fielder had shared a dugout about two miles from Caldwell near Bluff Creek. George Freeman, who had become a township constable in the last election, described McCarty as "about five feet ten . . . straight as a warrior, well formed ... and strikingly handsome." He had brown curly hair. Believed to be from Texas, he seemed well educated though he dressed in frontier clothes as did most settlers. Most important, he was known to be a skilled marksman.

Dan Fielder, from Pottawatomi County, Kansas to the north, was a respected settler who tried to avoid trouble as much as possible. Of medium build, he too dressed the part of a frontiersman.

One day in late March 1872, Mike McCarty headed to Caldwell for some fun. Late that night he returned to the dugout whiskey bent. At times like this he felt like fighting.

His partner Dan Fielder lay sleeping. McCarty rushed up to him, told him to get up and fight, then grabbed his hair and drug him out of bed. Fielder refused to fight. He wanted sleep. Ignoring McCarty's challenge, he returned to bed.

McCarty became infuriated. He again grabbed Fielder's hair and dragged him to the floor. Fielder had no choice. He traded punches with McCarty. It didn't last long. Fielder soon pounded McCarty to a bloody mess.

The next day McCarty's bruised and bloody face told others who won. Yet McCarty showed no hard feelings. After all, he'd initiated the confrontation.

A few days later, on Sunday, April 1, Mike McCarty rode into Caldwell and again hit the bottle. By now most settlers in the area knew McCarty's habits. Someone who had seen McCarty at the saloon rode by their dugout and informed Fielder about McCarty's condition. Fielder had no desire to fight McCarty again, so he went to John Reid's place on Fall Creek.

Later that night McCarty returned to his dugout fired up to fight. But all he found was an empty room. Determined to find Fielder, he returned to the saloon and asked friends where Fielder was. They told him.

McCarty planned his attack. He checked his pistol and wrapped a heavy blanket around his body before riding to John Reid's dugout.

When he arrived, he called out for Fielder. Someone inside yelled that Fielder was not there. McCarty called out again.

"Here I am," Fielder then answered. "Come in here if you want anything."

McCarty rushed inside to face Fielder's drawn gun. Fielder fired. McCarty's blanket stopped the force of the ball. McCarty fired back. The ball pierced Fielder's lung, killing him almost instantly. McCarty got on his horse and rode south into Indian Territory, where he hid out for the next several days.[28]

The next day, Caldwell held another township election. This temporarily distracted people from the incident. Also settlers classed the killing as self-defense since both parties had fired. But the town still didn't care much for Mike McCarty and McCarty knew it. So he made himself scarce to let sentiments cool down.

In the 1872 township election that day, George Freeman became a constable. This kept him in touch with the wildest element in the area. (When he later wrote a book about Caldwell and its surroundings, he based it on many of these first-hand experiences with outlaws).

Mike McCarty liked excitement and drinking, so he didn't stay away too long. When he felt he could no longer remain isolated, he decided to return to Caldwell. On Tuesday, April 9, a week after the elections and eight days after shooting Fielder, McCarty and a friend named Webb entered the town. They headed to the Cox and Epperson store and saloon where James M. Thomas had become proprietor after leasing out the store.

McCarty and Webb entered the store while a man named Doc Anderson, who had recently sold his store in Butler county, was bartering with Thomas. Anderson hoped to sell some goods left over from his store. Anderson happened to be wearing a top hat (known as a plug hat). He had recently won it in a card game in Wellington while on his way to Caldwell. A plug hat was seldom seen on the frontier. McCarty noticed it when he entered the store.

McCarty told Webb he'd like to shoot a hole through the hat. Webb told him to forget about it. When Anderson turned to show some of his goods to Thomas, McCarty shot toward Anderson. Instead of hitting the hat, McCarty put a hole through Anderson's head.

Again McCarty rode south. This time the town saw McCarty's gunplay as clear-cut murder. They formed a posse and headed after him. They knew that one of McCarty's favorite spots was the Last Chance Saloon surrounded by Bluff Creek to the south. He had close ties to the proprietor Curly Marshall and the outlaw element that frequented it.

Word quickly spread that McCarty knew the horse thieves who were lynched in Butler county back in 1870. Anderson, so the rumor said, had been one of the men who hunted down the eight victims of the vigilantes. So McCarty, people believed, had killed in revenge.

The vigilantes suspected McCarty had headed to Curly Marshall's ranch, the Last Chance, to hide out or get supplies before heading into Indian Territory. So that's where they headed.

About 15 to 20 vigilantes led by Dr. C.A. Rohrabacher, known as a rebel who spent time in an Iowa penitentiary, entered the Last Chance ranch area late that night. No moon shone. Curly Marshall may have been in Wichita at the time hiring prostitutes for his new dance hall. The men asked the acting ranch proprietor for permission to search the place for McCarty. The proprietor refused to let them.

The vigilantes left. Two or three rode back to Caldwell. They planned on returning with needed supplies to end the stand off.

Several others hid in a ravine about 200 yards north of the ranch area. The remaining men took positions behind the bluffs surrounding the Last Chance.

Sometime later the men who went to Caldwell returned with two pails of coal oil and bed quilts. Several men snuck up to the new frame dance hall. They soaked the bed quilts with oil, pinned the quilts to the building, and lit them.

The new frame building burst into flames. Moments later men rushed out, several rolling whiskey barrels. Both sides began firing. Several Last Chance men were injured. The vigilantes escaped injury, but they found no McCarty.

Next morning, someone handed Constable George Freeman a warrant for Mike McCarty's arrest. Freeman organized a posse and began searching. The posse searched all day with no success. When they returned to Caldwell they learned that the vigilantes knew McCarty's whereabouts. Freeman hurriedly led the posse south to catch up to the vigilantes.

Meanwhile two of the vigilantes had done undercover work. They went into Indian Territory, circled back, and rode up to the Last Chance from the Bluff Creek cattle crossing to the east, pretending to be cowboys on the trail north. They stopped for drinks.

They quickly got the drop on the two men attending the store. Soon other vigilantes joined them. The vigilantes, now in control of the ranch, waited for someone else to turn up that might lead them to McCarty. That's when they got lucky.

Busey Nicholson (or Boosey Nickleson) stopped at the ranch. He asked for a drink, then asked where Curly Marshall was. Nicholson said someone had ordered him to get $500 from Curly.

"Who gave you the order?" the vigilantes asked Nicholson. Nicholson refused to say. The vigilantes brought out a rope and gave Nicholson a choice. Talk or die, they said. Nicholson changed his mind. He told them the money was for McCarty, who had hid out near Deer Creek about 12 miles south.

Constable Freeman finally caught up with the vigilantes while they were still at the Last Chance. He too hoped track down McCarty. The two groups agreed to travel together south to Deer Creek starting at four a.m. next morning.

Freeman then headed home for some sleep. Next morning, April 11, he left Caldwell at three. When he reached the Last Chance, he found the vigilantes had already gone south. They later claimed they feared the longer they waited, the greater the chance McCarty would leave Deer Creek since Nicholson had never returned after saying he would.

Freeman headed south hoping to catch up with the vigilantes. Shortly he met some of the vigilantes returning. They filled him in with the latest news.

At Deer Creek the vigilantes said they found, as they feared, that McCarty had left the place. They then fanned out and searched further south.

Soon they spotted a stationary horse at a distance. They approached close enough to identify it as McCarty's. They then waited till dawn before they spotted McCarty sleeping on the ground by the horse.

McCarty was laying with his head on his saddle. He had tied a 30-foot rope from the horse to his saddle horn. The vigilantes surrounded him and called for his surrender.

McCarty jumped up and began firing a Sharps rifle while trying to work his way back to his horse. One of the vigilantes, Newt Williams, jumped between him and the horse and cut the rope. Some buckshot tore into McCarty's right hand. McCarty tried to fire a revolver with his left hand but realized his situation was hopeless. He surrendered.

The vigilantes argued over what to do next. Some wanted to hang McCarty, others to shoot him, and others to haul him back to Kansas for trial. Dan Fielder's brother happened to be among the vigilantes. When others asked him what he wanted, Fielder said they should take McCarty back for trial.

Someone else asked which gun McCarty had used to kill Dan Fielder. When told, this vigilante held it to McCarty's head and fired.

The vigilantes left McCarty's body where it was. Several days later, on Thursday, April 14, a group from Caldwell including B.W. Fox, Webb (McCarty's friend?), Robinson, and others buried the body.[29]

The Caldwell vigilantes killed two birds with one stone when they hunted down McCarty. They put a kink in the Last Chance's ability to take business away from Caldwell and they scared off a number of other horse thieves, at least for a while.

Curly Marshall was determined to rebuild. He went to Wichita, bought lumber for a new dance hall, and headed back to the Last Chance. As he traveled through Caldwell, he came face to face with Newt Williams. Marshall knew Williams' role as a vigilante. But Williams had no fear of Marshall. As Marshall rode by, Williams called out.

"Marshall, I want to see you."

Marshall stopped his wagon. Williams walked up to him.

"I understand, Mr. Marshall, you intend to kill me on sight," Williams said. Marshall scowled, ready to reach for his gun. But before either man could draw, others in the street jumped on them and wrestled away the weapons.

Curly Marshall got the message. The town made it clear he would no longer be welcome in the area.

Marshall turned his team of horses around and headed to the north part of Caldwell. There he settled all necessary business. He sold the Last Chance to Dave Terrill and returned the lumber for the dance hall to Wichita. He never again showed his face in Caldwell.

Dave Terrill kept the Last Chance going. Texans preferred it to saloons in Caldwell. And because of its location, it continued to attract the outlaw crowd.

The McCarty killings marked the beginning of Caldwell's Wild West cattle trail town reputation. Word spread that law took a vacation there. Headlines in a paper from the state capitol read:

"The Troubles in Sumner County. Vigilantes On The Rampage." The article told about the lynching of Mike McCarty of Caldwell and that of John D. Lynch in Wellington.

Though Lynch was accused of killing D.H. Maxfield in Wellington, Caldwell vigilantes hunted him down. Lynch probably didn't kill Maxfield. The shooting took place near the end of April. Two accounts from settlers in Wellington told similar stories. D.N. Caldwell, a young lawyer, and Joe Thralls, a lawman, remembered the affair years later.

According to Caldwell, when a prairie fire destroyed several of the settler's homes near Wellington, the town chose D.H. Maxfield to help raise funds for the vicitms' families. Maxfield and his young son came to town on Friday, April 26, for that reason.

That same day Jack Lynch, who lived in Wellington, along with Lew Hopkins, "Red Shirt," J.H. Dugdale, who ran a livery stable, and his assistant, Jesse Blissay, began drinking and gambling. These five continued this throughout the day and into the night. The way Thralls remembered it, two hunters, Smith and "Red Shirt" Blanchard, were with Lynch. The three men argued as they drank. They even threatened to shoot each other.

That night, Maxfield and his boy picked up food and clothes donations from J.R. Walter's store and Gifford's saloon to load on their wagon. As Maxfield carried the last load from Gifford's, Lynch, "Red Shirt," and Smith (or Hopkins), still arguing at this saloon, began shooting.

According to Thralls, Lynch went out the front door and hid, waiting for Smith to exit. When Smith came out, Lynch shot at him. The bullet hit the doorframe before hitting Smith in the chest. The bullet stopped at Smith's clothing.

Lynch thought he'd killed Smith, so he ran. While running away, he accidentally shot his own feet. Meantime, Smith sought revenge. He ran out the south door and saw a man he thought was Lynch. He shot before realizing the man was Maxfield. To protect themselves, Smith, along with "Red Shirt," claimed Lynch had shot Maxfield.

Wellington Constable Dan William Jones had no trouble arresting Lynch, who was being treated by Dr. E.P. Richey at the Cleveland hotel. But Jones doubted he could hold the prisoner for very long.

Next day, Saturday, April 27, Caldwell vigilantes began congregating in Wellington. Acting Sheriff Andrew A. Jordan devised a plan to hide Lynch from the vigilantes. This worked for a while, but the vigilantes, led by J.W. Reynolds, found Lynch on Sunday, April 28. Reynolds claimed Lynch was a known horse thief, so whether they could prove he killed Maxfield or not made little difference.

That day the vigilantes got Judge Reuben Riggs to make out Lynch's will. Later that evening the Caldwell vigilantes hanged Lynch.

"No one doubts but that McCarty and Lynch both richly deserved punishment for their crimes," the Topeka paper said. "But for a gang composed mainly of outlaws themselves to murder a man and leave his body on the prairie and then hang a wounded prisoner is a system of civilization which ultimately ruins any country on earth."

Another article in the same paper saw other motives working in the McCarty affair. "It is said that the Caldwell roughs made McCarty outrages a mere excuse for ridding themselves of the rival store situated at the river crossing about a mile from Caldwell, which was seriously militating against their trade," it said.[30]

The Lynch execution following the McCarty incident got Kansas Governor James Harvey's attention. He sent a letter to Sumner County acting sheriff Andrew A. Jordan offering military assistance. Jordan held off. Lucky for Caldwell no more killings took place in May. Caldwell leaders believed the vigilantes' swift treatment of horse thieves and murderers did the trick. But next month brought more trouble.

"It was the last chance to get a drink."

Wednesday, June 5, 1872 proved to be eventful for Caldwell. Around nine a.m. Constable George Freeman rode north out of town with a cowboy. Freeman had a summons to serve on a Texas cattleman named Oliver. The cowboy had gone to court to get Oliver to pay him in coin as their contract stated. The cow camp was about 12 miles off.

Freeman arrived at noon. He told the cowboy with him to stay behind to prevent trouble. Freeman then confronted Oliver. Oliver surprised Freeman. He welcomed the lawman and invited him and the cowboy to dinner. The three men ate, then headed back to Caldwell. They arrived in late afternoon.

◊

Before Freeman, Oliver, and the cowboy arrived in Caldwell, Milton Freeman, George's younger brother, happened to drive George's wagon with a team of his horses to a haystack a couple of miles away. He had left at four p.m.

Milton had gone about a mile when two men rode up and asked him where they could ford the creek. Milton turned to show them, and they drew their revolvers. They took the wagon and forced him to go with them. They rode west till midnight, then made Milton get out and walk home.

Young Freeman walked east. At three in the morning, he came to Major Andrew Drumm's ranch (near present day Kiowa).

Drumm listened to Freeman's story, gave him breakfast, then gave him a horse to ride back to Caldwell.

◊

Back in Caldwell, George Freeman arrived too late to take Oliver to court. That meant the cattleman had to stay overnight.

Next morning, Thursday, June 6, some of Oliver's cowboys rode into town and told him of more trouble. At seven p.m. the evening before, one of Oliver's cowboys killed another in a fight. And Oliver's cattle scattered.

Oliver quickly paid his disgruntled employee in coin, paid court costs, and Freeman released him. The cattleman rode back to camp hoping to solve his problems.

◊

Shortly after that, Milton Freeman rode into town and told George about the stolen wagon and horses. George also received an anonymous letter. It named the horse thieves. It also said the thieves were headed to Albert Henry Boyd's ranch near Larned. Boyd's place was believed to be a haven for horse thieves.

Freeman had no problem finding volunteers. The posse left at nine a.m.[31] Early that afternoon they spotted wagon tracks and horseshoe prints. Freeman recognized the prints. He had shoed the horse. The posse followed the tracks through the afternoon. They stopped and slept outdoors for that night before continuing.

By the second day the posse decided to split up for a better chance of finding the thieves. Shortly after that all the groups except for Freeman's quit the search.

Freeman's group included seven men – Ballard Dixon, Asa Overall, Jim McGuire, Sullivan, Dobbs, and Franklin.[32] On Saturday, June 8, Freeman and his men ran across a day-old camp of the thieves. The discovery spurred them on. But they were low on food and water. They killed an antelope and had to drink from a buffalo wallow.

That night it rained. Next day, Sunday, June 9, they had trouble following the tracks because of the mud. They continued for about 20 miles when they noticed the tracks looked fresher. They sped up, running their horses for about five miles before stopping for a needed rest about a mile and a half from the Arkansas River.

They hid in a ravine at their elevated position so people on the trail in the valley below could not spot them. Freeman contrived a camouflage of weeds tied together. He crawled to the top of a hill with the weeds in front of him to view the valley.

He soon spotted a wagon and three horses grazing nearby. Freeman's party waited till dark before moving closer, quietly approaching through a ravine to make sure they had the right wagon. They then returned to their camp for the night.

Before daybreak next morning, Monday, June 10, they spread out and crawled up to within 50 feet of the wagon and horses. They hunched in 18-inch tall grass, waiting for the right chance to surprise the thieves. When daylight broke, Freeman stood and called out for them to surrender. At the third call, one man raised his head above the wagon. Freeman yelled for the other thief to show himself. The posse soon found out the other one had left.

The captured man said his partner had crossed the river and gone to Boyd's ranch. He said his partner was Tom Smith (real name Tom Ford) and he was Dalton.[33]

George Freeman and his men waited in hiding for Tom Ford to return. Around 10 a.m. they spotted him at a distance.

When Ford reached the Arkansas, he swam across with his horse. He then rode slowly toward the wagon, but hesitated before reaching it. He was still several hundred yards from the posse.

Suddenly one of the posse stood up. Freeman quickly jumped up and called out for Ford to surrender. Ford wheeled around and spurred his horse away. Freeman chased him. Ford headed for the hills. Freeman figured Ford would draw him in only to bushwhack him if he followed. But another posse member beat Ford to the hills and forced him to take another route. Ford crossed the river and sped away. The posse followed, losing ground as they went. They soon lost sight of him but continued on till they reached Fort Larned.

They went to the quartermaster's store to buy food. There they overheard a soldier talking about Tom Ford. Indians had attacked Ford. Wounded, Ford went to the fort and asked for help to chase down the Indians.

Freeman also found out Ford went to Boyd's ranch three miles east. Freeman went to the fort's commanding officer and asked for help to catch Ford. A sergeant with six soldiers and an old scout left with Freeman and his posse.

Two miles from the ranch Freeman spotted a horseback rider just leaving Boyd's place. He told the sergeant and three soldiers to follow the rider while the rest continued on to the ranch.

At the ranch, Freeman got no information from Boyd's bartender. The posse searched the building, then left to return to Fort Larned. About a mile from the fort they ran into the sergeant and his party, who had captured Tom Ford.

When they got back to the fort, Tom Ford complained to the commanding officer that Freeman had no right to hold him. Freeman showed the officer his commission as a deputy U.S. marshal. The officer accepted his credentials and had the blacksmith shop make shackles to hold the prisoners for their trip back to Caldwell.

They left on Monday, June 10. When they crossed the Arkansas River, Tom Ford nearly drowned. Being shackled hand and foot didn't help.

At six p.m. they arrived at the place they caught Dalton. There they camped for the night. Several men stayed on guard since they were afraid Ford's and Dalton's friends would try to help them escape. Each person in the posse had a shotgun and two revolvers. Two on guard had Winchesters rifles. Nothing happened that night.

Next morning they hooked up the wagon and headed to Caldwell. Part of their food, their hardtack, was ruined when they crossed the Arkansas the day before, so they only had bacon to eat. That evening they camped by some water since they knew there was a stretch of dry land ahead.

Next day, Wednesday, June 12, they traveled all morning hoping to find another stream to drink from. They were also out of food. At noon they found a buffalo wallow. They used a prickly pear leaf to clean out some of the mud before drinking the water.

They continued east till nearly dark, when they camped near a branch of the Chikaskia. Though two guards stayed on duty all night, next morning the men discovered Dalton had escaped.

R.M. Johnston, a boyhood friend of Ford's, years later said that one of the guards, Asa Overall, grew to like Tom Ford. Overall at one point hinted to Ford that he might let him escape. Overall told Johnston that Ford refused the offer because he was afraid of getting Overall in trouble.[34] Freeman tried to track down Dalton for a while, but soon gave up.

This day, Thursday, June 13, dragged by. It had been two days since the men had eaten. Their luck returned when they discovered a cattle camp.

The posse stayed at a distance while Freeman went to the camp and asked for food. Freeman had to prove he was a deputy U.S. marshal before the boss herder agreed to let Freeman and his men eat with them. Refreshed, the men continued till they reached Caldwell at four p.m. One account said the posse stopped at the Last Chance saloon when Tom Ford told Freeman he would buy everyone drinks since he knew his end was near.[35]

Getting Ford to Caldwell didn't end Freeman's problems. People in town were up in arms. Freeman hauled Ford to the upstairs of James M. Thomas' store for safekeeping. All agreed to conduct a quick preliminary hearing.

Milton Freeman identified Tom Ford as one of the thieves. Ford confessed. He wrote a letter to his brother Sewell (alias Charlie Smith) in Wichita sending him $20 (or $40?) because he didn't expect to survive this ordeal. Justice of the Peace Dr. B.W. Fox ordered Freeman to take the prisoner to Wellington immediately. Freeman complied.

Six men, including Freeman, guarded Ford in a wagon as they headed to Wellington.
A few miles northeast of Caldwell, near Ryland's Ford on the Chikaskia River, vigilantes ambushed the guards and took Ford. They threatened to kill the guards if they tried to follow them. According to a later story, the only guard to put up any resistance in trying to protect Ford was Dan Carter.[36]

After the vigilantes left, Freeman and the other guards headed to Wellington to report what happened. They arrived at sunrise (Friday, June 14) and headed to the sheriff's office. Freeman told the sheriff what happened.

The guards ate some breakfast. They left Wellington at 10 a.m. to return to Caldwell. In the middle of the afternoon they arrived at the Chikaskia River. There they viewed Tom Ford's body hanging from an elm tree.[37]

For the next two years Constable George Freeman received continual threats from Tom Ford's older brother, Sewell (alias Charlie Smith). The threats took their toll.

A fellow settler, Sol King, years later remembered "Sewell Ford, alias Charles Smith, still continued to hang around Caldwell, making threats of vengeance on Freeman, who was a home loving peaceful sort of a chap, entirely too peaceful to have ever been elected as constable. The threats also worried Mrs. Freeman until she was almost a nervous wreck."[38]

Sewell Ford usually hung around the Last Chance Saloon when he was in the Caldwell area. Though Dave Terrill owned the Last Chance, A.C. McLean, who lived nearby, usually ran it. In the first issue of a new Wellington paper, the editor told of visiting Caldwell in September. "After staying in Caldwell over night," he said, "we rode to McLean's 'ranch' one mile south of Caldwell where we were joined by the jovial Mack himself, and we all took a trip to the Indian Territory one half mile away."[39]

In April 1874 Terrill sold the Last Chance to Hank Zuber and opened a restaurant in town called the Fort Worth.[40] But McLean continued to run the Last Chance.

The area between the Last Chance and Caldwell became a popular spot. Gamblers placed bets on horse races there. Rough characters with something to hide usually congregated near Bluff Creek and frequented the Last Chance.

Cowboy Duel

Reporters had no way of knowing how often cowboys met their end in gunfights or other violent deaths. Sometimes reporters received only sketchy information.

An incident that happened in late June or early July barely made the papers. Caldwell Constable George Freeman told of two cowboys who spent their day drinking in Caldwell. They left the saloon late at night. As they rode back to their cattle camp a mile or so north of town, they argued.

That night cowboys at the camp heard two shots. They figured the cowboys returning from town were letting off steam. Next morning the camp cook noticed the two cowboys lying on the ground a short distance off. He assumed they were sleeping off their hangover. When he completed breakfast, one of the cowboys from camp went out to wake them. The cowboy found two dead bodies with a bullet in each[41]

◊

Trail herds reached their zenith in the summer. Hundreds of cowboys passing by Caldwell in the 1872 summer celebrated. Newspapers could not keep track of all that happened. In August, the Wichita paper listed the 1871 cattle traffic through Caldwell as compared to that of 1872 up to the first week in July. In 1871, the number was 315,726 as compared to 240,311 for 1872. The cattle for 1871 totaled from 600,000 to 700,000. Total for 1872 came to about 300,000 to 400,000. Though the 1872 number was impressive, the number for 1871 would never be topped.[42]

A Year to Grow

The year 1873 brought changes to Caldwell. Settlers hoped to change the town's image from a primitive cattle trail trading post to a town that would attract farm families.

Caldwell formed a school district on September 21, 1872. By 1873 they built a $1,200 20 by 30 foot frame schoolhouse. That year the Methodist Church provided a circuit-riding preacher to visit Caldwell regularly. Rev. J.P. Harsen organized a Presbyterian Church and Rev. J.B. Rideout became its first pastor.[43]

A mail route from Wichita ran through Caldwell and all the way to Fort Sill, Indian Territory. Dr. O.G. Given, who traveled on the stage in April 1873, described his experience going through Sumner County.

"We were detained at Wellington until Tuesday the 4th when we took the stage out from Wichita," he said. "An afternoon's ride over the beautiful prairies of the southern part of Sumner County landed us in Caldwell in time to see the king of day sink himself beneath the western horizon.

"Caldwell is truly a frontier town, as a sign on the last house we passed before passing into the Indian Territory would indicate. On one side the sign reads Last Chance, on the other, First Chance. As I saw nothing very inviting about the appearance of the house or the surroundings, I was at a loss to know what it meant, and so I interrogated the driver. His reply was that it was the last chance to get a drink."[44]

Caldwell's leading businessman C.H. Stone held a different view of the town. While visiting Wichita in April, he spoke of Caldwell in glowing terms. He said he was looking forward to the coming cattle trade through Caldwell on its way to Wichita.

By 1873, though, cattle drives were increasingly heading toward Dodge City. Settlers were filling up land around Caldwell. Farmers complained about Texas fever spread by the cattle drives. If this trend continued, the future looked bleak for Caldwell. Still 400,000 to 450,000 cattle passed through town.

Citizens held out one hope for the future - a railroad. If Caldwell could convince a railroad to locate there, the town could still attract cattle drives and receive the business it brought.

In October, the Wellington paper discussed having the Atchison, Topeka, and Santa Fe railroad extend their line to Caldwell. "From personal knowledge we are fortunately able . . . to corroborate the statement . . . in regard to the superior excellence of the grazing grounds in the Territory south of Caldwell," it said. "The range is unlimited, and with Caldwell as a railroad terminus, it will become the great cattle shipping point of the whole county."[45]

But as much as Caldwell boosters hoped for a better image in 1873, the town's reputation remained. An incident in November confirmed this.

On Tuesday, November 4, Sumner County acting sheriff Andrew A. Jordan, along with deputies W.H. McClelland, A.W. Terrell, and a man named Nicholson, arrested Charlie King and Adelbert Haskins in Caldwell for stealing a team of horses and wagon. But King and Haskins were not locals. They had committed their crime in Winterset, Iowa.

"John S. Taylor had followed the thieves from Winterset, Iowa," the Wellington paper said. "He succeeded in striking their trail in Missouri, tracked them into and through Nebraska, followed their devious wanderings through northern Kansas, crossed the K.P. [Kansas Pacific] road at Russell, and thence to Great Bend on the Arkansas River. . . From Great Bend the thieves . . . went to Medicine Lodge."[46] Then they headed to Caldwell, believing it to be a sanctuary for outlaws.

In spite of this negative press, Caldwellites remained hopeful. Cattle drives, though expected to decrease in coming years, continued to wind their way through town. But even C.H. Stone hedged his bets on Caldwell's future when he opened a trading post in Indian Territory.[47]

4

"The Indian excitement involves the interest of the state."

Caldwell citizens continued to hope for a large chunk of the cattle business for the coming spring and summer. They looked for any positive signs to confirm this hope. In March, the Wellington paper put the best face on Caldwell's future that year.

"True, at this time of the year Caldwell people do not expect much in the way of business because, being sensible people they know that this is not the time of year for it," it said, "but in a few weeks the music of the 'cow boys' song will be heard on [the] trail as he brings the long horned bovines from their native pastures in Texas. Then will business in earnest begin and as before mentioned, our people being sensible, they are preparing for the busy time coming."[48]

The Wichita paper quoted cattleman James Bryden as to what he expected in the coming season. "In my opinion, and from observation, I believe the cattle men are less divided now than in former years on this question [of where the cattle will be headed]," he said. "Very few will attempt to drive to Ellsworth this year, and only those destined for western territories will think of passing Wichita."[49]

While Caldwell businessmen had the cattle trade primarily on their minds, they were blindsided by several unexpected events in July. Signs of these coming troubles showed up earlier.

Dodge City, Kansas, and Fort Sill, Indian Territory played key roles in the gathering storm of trouble for those who lived on the southern border of Kansas.

By 1873 the number of buffaloes had thinned out in and around Dodge City. Hunters knew they were in trouble when their own number sometimes exceeded that of the buffaloes.

That fall buffalo hunters Wright Mooar and John Webb came to Dodge City with news that buffalo herds remained thick in the Texas panhandle. Hunters paid attention. They weighed risks against benefits.

Everyone in that area risked raids from Indians at any time. Bands of Comanches and Kiowas often slipped away from their reservations and hunted buffalo there. These Indians hated the Dodge City buffalo hunters above everyone else because of their wasteful and massive killing of the Indian's main source of food.

Wright Mooar and another hunter, Steel Frazier, ended up asking Fort Dodge commanding officer Major Richard Irving Dodge his opinion about the declining buffalo herds around Dodge. "Boys," he said, "if I were a buffalo hunter, I would hunt where the buffaloes are."[50] This told them to head south.

In September, brothers John and Wright Mooar with four teams and 10 men for skinning and hauling headed south from Dodge City for better hunting grounds. They stopped at several places on the way and hunted.

Other hunters followed their lead. In March 1874 merchant A.C. "Charlie" Myers headed to the panhandle with 50 men and 30 wagons full of goods. Myers and most of the other hunters eventually settled by the South Canadian River near the old site of Adobe Walls. There they built several picket houses and stores to establish a trading post.

Cheyennes, Comanches, and Kiowas took notice. Commanche medicine man Isatai (Little Wolf) spoke to several bands of Indians who met for a Sun Dance in June near Fort Sill. He promised victory for the group if they attacked the buffalo hunters at Adobe Walls.

"The Indian excitement involves the interest of the state."

Early Saturday morning, June 27, 1874, several hundred of these Indians attacked Adobe Walls' 28 occupants. The Indians were no match for the buffalo hunters' powerful rifles. The Indians did kill three of the hunters. But Billy Dixon showed what the big guns could do when he picked off one of the enemy from nearly a mile away. After several days, the Indians gave up and rode off.[51]

This incident increased the Indians' frustration. They began conducting raids on isolated settlers on the southern plains, killing a number in southern Kansas. They also attacked freighters working between Fort Sill and Caldwell on the Chisholm Trail.

People differed sharply on who or what to blame for the Indians' behavior. Government officials and Indian agents often blamed whites for exploiting the Indians primary source of existence. They believed white horse thieves and murderers preyed on reservation Indians. They also believed government contractors often provided poor meat and inadequate provisions to the powerless wards of the state. Whatever else was behind the increasing presence of roving Indian bands who attacked isolated settlers, Indian agents believed the root cause centered on the way whites treated them.

Not surprisingly, settlers and newspaper editors blamed "Quaker agents" for allowing Indians to leave their reservations and roam the country freely only to kill and scalp homesteaders, traders, and freighters. Often the government hired Indian agents to help in peace making, or at least to offer their peacekeeping skills. Most of the agents were Quakers.

Since these agents believed in peace above all else, they sometimes turned their heads away when Indians left the reservation to hunt, sympathizing with the Indians' plight. But this also created a problem to isolated farmers and freighters who ended up being the victims of these Indians' wrath.

John D. Miles, the Cheyenne/Arapaho agent at the Darlington Agency south of Caldwell was no exception to the stereotypical agent. He too was a Quaker. And he seemed to sympathize more with the Indians than with the settlers.

Shortly after the Adobe Walls fight, Caldwell citizens heard
about Indian attacks near towns west of them. July 2 headlines in
the Wellington paper read, "Indian Raid. Eight Men Killed and
Scalped in Barbour County. Settlers abandon their homes and rush
into the towns for protection. Cheyennes on the War Path."

This article listed several incidents. It said Cheyennes stole
horses and wounded two men at Kiowa. Four miles outside of
Medicine Lodge they killed and scalped a man named Kime. A few
miles west of Medicine Lodge they killed and scalped two others.
Another group of Indians killed two men at a ranch at the head of
Mule Creek. Indians also killed and scalped a boy named Cone (or
Coon).[52]

Major H.T. Beman made a report to the Topeka paper about
people he interviewed in early July. Beman heard about more
killings when he talked to James Fay, an express messenger for
Southwestern Stage Company, which ran between Wichita and Fort
Sill.

"Mr. Fay says that the settlers about the agencies are
apprehensive of a general massacre," Beman reported. "[The
settlers] are few in number, and unless under the very eye of the
agency, are without protection. The Indians have killed four of the
horses of the Southwestern stage company within the last few days,
and Mr. Fay has witnessed one murder and scalping committed by
them.

"The facts of the latest occurrence were as follows: Last
Thursday [June 30] on the way in from Fort Sill, when the stage was
a short distance from Red Fork station in the Seminole nation, he
[Fay] saw from his stage a party of Indians ride up on to a
defenseless man, murder him, and sweep on out of sight. Hastening
to the spot he found the man killed and scalped lying in the road.
His name was William Watkins, and he was brought to Red Fork
station and buried."[53]

On Saturday, July 4, Caldwell residents heard rumors that 500
Indians were headed to town and were only five miles south. Many
didn't know whether to believe it or not. It did put people on edge

as they celebrated Independence Day. One newspaper article made light of the rumor about Indians when townspeople spooked for other reasons.

"But lo! The romance of border life was knocked into pi," it said, "when it was ascertained that instead of being the dreaded savage decked in paint and feathers, it was a very innocent looking herd of Texas cattle."[54]

Two days later Caldwell residents did panic. Monday afternoon, July 6, Agent John D. Miles, head of the Darlington (Cheyenne/Arapaho) Agency about 110 miles south of Caldwell rode into Caldwell with bad news. Indians were on the warpath, Miles said. About 65 miles south of Caldwell he had come upon the body of Pat Hennessey. Hennessey was tied to a wagon wheel and burned alive. He and three others, George Fant, Thomas Calaway, and Ed Cook, had been killed on Saturday, July 4.[55]

When Caldwell citizens heard Agent Miles' report of murdered freighters, many panicked. Miles' four-horse stage soon headed for Wellington. They arrived between midnight and one a.m. (Tuesday, July 7). Miles told Wellington town leaders of Indian danger at Caldwell before continuing on to Wichita on his way to Fort Leavenworth.

Miles' family and others, including two brothers, J.C. and Lou Hopkins, who operated Pond Creek Station (Sewell's Ranch) 25 miles south of Caldwell, traveled on the same stage. J.C. and Lou Hopkins got off the stage at Caldwell. They were on a desperate mission.

A supply train led by a man named Laflin waited at the Pond Creek Station before heading south. Laflin's men refused to leave the Pond Creek ranch without receiving reinforcements. Laflin oversaw 17 wagons containing 86,000 pounds of freight. But the 19 men in his crew had only three guns among them.[56] They feared being raided by Indians if they headed further south. The Hopkins brothers had agreed to go to Caldwell and bring back arms and ammunition for the 19 men to protect themselves.

Wellington town leader William P. Hackney organized a posse
to head south to protect Caldwell settlers. Hackney, 31, a state
representative, had no trouble attracting some of the most seasoned
and skilled men for the job. Among those in his group were C.S.
Brodbent, A.W. Sherman, L.K. Meyers, J.A. Kirk, T.J. Riley, James
Stipp, Joseph M. Thralls, his brother William E. "Elzy" Thralls, and
John H. Folks. Hackney headed to Caldwell with about 20 men.

Towns all along the southern Kansas border panicked, but
especially Caldwell. Indians liked to attack freighters on the
Chisholm Trail more than any other place. Settlers living south of
Caldwell along Bluff Creek packed up and ran north to Caldwell or
on to Wellington or even Wichita.

Travelers all along the Chisholm Trail had good reason to panic,
and they did. Most headed straight to Caldwell for protection.
Among them were some of the wildest characters around.

"Caldwell was full of freighters and troops yesterday [Monday,
July 6]," said the Topeka paper. "There is a regular stampede up the
trail."[57]

Even desperate characters and suspected horse thieves, fearing
for their lives, headed north. Soon a number of them congregated in
Caldwell.

"The country around here is full of horse thieves, the town of
Caldwell and the timber of Bluff Creek being a sort of refuge for
them," said the Topeka paper. "Bully Brooks, formerly of Dodge
City, and a number of ruffians of that kidney, have been driven in
from the Territory by fear of Indians, and are hanging around the
cavalry and militia, casting wistful eyes at their horses."[58]

The Wellington home militia group arrived at Caldwell later that
morning (July 7) after passing a number of fleeing homesteaders.
They noticed the town full of excited settlers along with cowboys
and shady characters. Among the characters was Billy Brooks,
Sewell Ford (alias Charlie Smith), and the Moore brothers. The
Moores, according to Hackney and Thralls, headed up the gang.

William L. "Billy" Brooks became Newton, Kansas' first city
marshal in 1872. Later that year he served as a lawman in

50

"The Indian excitement involves the interest of the state."

Ellsworth. But by December he had moved to Dodge City as a buffalo hunter. There he shot and killed a man. By then he had the reputation as a bully who was ready to shoot first and talk later. But another buffalo hunter named Kirk Jordan backed him down with one shot from a buffalo gun in March 1873. A few months later he was living by Bluff Creek south of Caldwell with his wife. Those around him suspected he was a horse and mule thief.[59]

Sewell "Charlie Smith" Ford, as mentioned earlier, often hung around the Last Chance Saloon. At one time he owned a trader ranch at Ninnescah crossing (near present day Clearwater). He made frequent trips to Wichita. His reputation as a horse thief preceded him. Sewell blamed George Freeman for Tom Ford's death and threatened to kill him.

Bill Hackney and his men in Caldwell ran into the Hopkins brothers who were collecting arms and ammunition for their journey south. When the brothers told the Wellington men about heading back to Pond Creek Station that morning, the Wellington men feared for the brothers' safety. Hackney and his group saw danger not only from Indians, but also from the suspected horse thieves such as Brooks and Ford.

Joe Thralls closely watched these characters. "They were worse than the Indians and when we found a bunch of them eating breakfast at Caldwell it made us want to turn the Indian hunt into a horse-thief capturing expedition," he said.[60]

As the Hopkins left town, Hackney and his men continued to monitor the Moore brothers' gang. The Moore gang watched the Hopkins leave. Shortly after that they too left.

Hackney quickly made up his mind. He and most of his men mounted up and followed the gang, watching out for Indians at the same time.

Joe Thralls, who served as a constable in Wellington, had a three-band Sharp's needle gun with him. Bill Hackney remembered the situation. "Joe Thralls had borrowed a gun," he said, "a very fine one recently purchased by Frank Bates, who reluctantly gave it to him and with the express condition that he would return it."[61]

Others in the group had pistols and Spencer rifles. But most settlers prized the Sharps rifle above any other weapon.

As Hackney's group rode south, they kept their eyes on the Moore gang ahead of them. Ahead of the Moore gang rode the Hopkins with their wagon full of supplies.

The Hopkins, the Moore gang, and Hackney's group all stopped to rest at Pole Cat Ranch (near present day Renfrow) about 12 miles south of Caldwell. Then things got serious.

Hackney remembered what happened. A leader of the Moore gang walked over to the Hackney's men with a demand. He wanted more weapons and especially the rifle Thralls had. He said his men needed the rifle and other weapons for protection on their trip to Fort Sill, and promised to return the arsenal on their way back.

Thralls politely refused to loan them the Sharps, explaining he had borrowed it with the promise of returning it immediately after returning. He even said the Moore gang could borrow some of the other rifles.

The leader of the gang went back to his men and told them what happened. One of the others, a big Texan, jumped up and said, "Hell, what's the use of bothering with them? Let's take that gun and the others."[62]

Bill Hackney responded without hesitation, according to Joe Thralls. "I have heard Bill cuss a good many times, but never heard him do as artistic a job as he did that day," Thralls said. "The rest of us were no mollycoddles, but Bill's language almost made us shudder. In substance, Bill spoke as follows: 'If you ----- sons of ------- want that gun, come and get it, but I want to say that if one of you makes a move in that direction, there will be a lot of dead horse thieves left here on the ground for buzzard feed.'"[63]

The Moore gang backed off. They mounted up and headed south without their desired rifle or other weapons.

The Hopkins made it safely to Pond Creek. Hackney and his men headed back to Caldwell, where they tried to sooth the nerves of fearful settlers. They told the settlers there was no sign of raiding Indians. Then they headed back to Wellington.

52

"The Indian excitement involves the interest of the state."

Shortly after that another posse from Belle Plaine entered Caldwell saying they would help protect them. Caldwell told them to go home. The Wellington group had already done what was needed.

Caldwell citizens now turned their efforts to fighting horse thief gangs, not Indians. They determined to find the leading gang members and put an end to their thievery.

But fear of raiding Indians depopulated part of southern Kansas. Cheyenne-Arapaho Agent John Miles told Kansas Governor Thomas Osborne about the Indian problem and fleeing settlers. Governor Osborn paid attention. "The Indian excitement which now prevails in southern Kansas seriously involves the interests of the state, in the matter of immigration especially," said the Topeka paper.

Governor Osborn asked for help from the military. Soon government officers helped organize a militia to protect southern Kansas settlers. They started by choosing experienced frontiersmen to lead groups of militiamen.

"Captain Morris, the adjutant general, arrived in [Wichita] yesterday [Friday, July 10] to raise a company of mounted militia," the same paper said. "He came to Wichita because here are obtainable the right sort of men for the purpose—frontiersmen, scouts, and old Indian fighters—men of nerve, coolness, judgment, and indomitable physical endurance.

"He might have recruited a hundred such, but he contented himself with enlisting forty picked men, who furnish their own horses. They will be armed with Sharps carbines and revolvers, of course, and provided with rations and subsistence.

"The object of this expedition, which Captain Morris accompanies to Caldwell where he will make his headquarters, is to scout along the southwestern border and find out if there are or are to be any fears to be had of Indian outrages, and to engage any party which may be found. The Captain's object is to satisfy the people of the state that no danger is to be feared and to restore confidence."

53

"The militia company is officered as follows, the officers being elected by vote at a meeting yesterday: S. M. Tucker, captain; Mike Meagher, 1st lieutenant; and Cash Henderson, 2nd lieutenant.

"Mr. Tucker is an old soldier, formerly a resident of Fort Scott, and now a practicing lawyer in this city. Mike Meagher is a famous scout in the southwest, formerly marshal of Wichita, and a terror to the longhaired, pistol-shooting gentry from Texas and the Territory. Mr. Henderson is a salesman in a dry goods store in this city, but a good man for the position notwithstanding the peaceful character of his occupation. This small army moves out at nine o'clock this morning and will camp out about seventeen miles from the city, where they will overtake the three companies of infantry under command of Captain Ovenshine.[64]

◊

During the time Indian raids increasingly threatened southern Kansas, horse thieves in the Caldwell area increased their activity. Thievery had been on the rise for some time.

"Horses and cattle by the thousands have been spirited away during the past three years," said the Wellington paper. "The Texas cattle trail has especially been infested by these outlaws, and the ranches of the traders have furnished suitable headquarters for the leaders of the gang, and safe asylums for the thieves and their plunder."[65]

But part of the reason thievery increased rapidly in 1874 could have been greater opportunity. The thieves saw an opportunity to use Indian raids as a cover for their activity. And thieves had stronger incentive than that – a bigger paycheck than usual. They found a lucrative employer in the summer of 1874.

That summer Vail and Company outbid the Southwestern Stage line for a U.S. mail contract for delivering mail between Caldwell and Fort Sill. The contract went into effect on July 1. Southwestern figured they needed a way to get back that business. Behind the scenes they hired members of a horse thief band.

"The Indian excitement involves the interest of the state."

By late June, Vail prepared for their new business. "Mr. [L.T.] Williamson, agent for Vail & Co., the contractors on mail route from here [Caldwell] to Fort Sill, passed through yesterday [Wednesday, June 24] with fourteen mules and five gigs or sulkies to stock the route," said the Wellington paper. "Our postmaster informs me that after the first of July five mail routes will be in operation to this place [Caldwell] from Wellington, London, Peace, A.T. & S.F. railroad, Chetopa, the longest route in the state, and Fort Sill, I.T."[66]

Southwestern offered the thieves more than enough money to interest them in stealing Vail's livestock. But they had to work fast. July 1st was fast approaching. By late June Vail's stock disappeared at an alarming rate.

"Four mules and a horse, the latter belonging to A.E. Fletcher, were stolen from Judd Calkins' livery barn in Caldwell last Monday night [June 29]," said the Wellington paper. "So adroitly was the theft accomplished that the horse was taken from the very side of young Fletcher, who was sleeping in the barn at the time. The mules belonged to Vail & Co. and had just been sent down to stock the mail line between Caldwell and Fort Sill. This is another of a series of thefts perpetrated by an organized band of outlaws who have so far escaped detection themselves and who have succeeded in so effectively concealing the stock that no trace of them is left behind to guide pursuit."[67]

Clearly Caldwell had its hands full. Would lawless gangs triumph and chase off the farmers and merchants to safer climes or would the town find a way to combat this outlawry?

"His feet were swaying to and fro..."

By the first week of July 1874, nearly all of Vail and Company's stock was gone. This success emboldened the thieves. They began to think of themselves as invincible.

Vail and Company had to stop them or go out of business. They offered $300 reward for anyone who could track down the thieves and return the stolen animals. Problem was, no one seemed to have any idea where the thieves hid out. Unless someone came up with a good lead, Vail's reward would never be used.

One man in Caldwell knew. A.C. "Mack" McLean, who ran the Last Chance Saloon south of Caldwell, had an inside track when it came to information about horse thieves. He saw them come and go daily. He heard their talk.

If the outlaws didn't completely trust him, neither did they fear him. They figured he wouldn't repeat what he heard if he wanted to stay alive. They figured wrong.

McLean overheard who was stealing livestock and why. Though fearful of what might happen should the outlaws find out, McLean told Caldwell doctor and druggist P.J.M. Burkett what he knew. He also told Burkett where the outlaws were headed. On July 15 Burkett relayed the information, promising not to reveal his source. He told town leader A.M. Colson he should organize a posse and go after horse thieves who would pass by the H.J. Devore farm (12 miles west of Caldwell) next morning at nine. McLean believed the thieves were headed to Larned or Fort Dodge.

Colson rode to the Chikaskia River north of Caldwell where settlers had suffered heavy losses from horse thieves. Several men joined his posse. Before heading west after the thieves, Colson contacted Sheriff John G. Davis, asking for help, then spent the night near the Chikaskia before heading out. Next morning the posse rode west to the Devore ranch hoping to run into the outlaws. They didn't. But they did meet up with Sheriff Davis' posse from Wellington.

The men found out the outlaws passed by the ranch earlier. The posse stayed long enough to eat breakfast before heading northwest along the Ellsworth Trail. After a few days travel, only nine men remained on the chase, four from Wellington and five from Caldwell.

Sheriff Davis' group included Joe Thralls, John Botkin, and Neal [Thomas C.] Gatliff.[68] Colson's group included W.B. King, Frank Barrington, Alex Williamson, John Williams, and a man named Force. These 10 men continued toward the Fort Dodge area determined to find the thieves.[69]

After leaving Devore's ranch, the going got rough for the posse since they took few provisions thinking they would catch up quickly with the thieves. Instead they lost the trail, split up for awhile to search for a lead, and eventually ran into a boy who remembered seeing some men as described by the posse. The boy said the outlaws were at Sand Creek 15 miles west.

There the posse picked up the outlaws' tracks. But by then the sun had set. The posse, dead tired and hungry, rested for the night. Next morning they followed the outlaw trail as fast as they could though their horses had little left. They'd already covered more than 200 miles in the last several days.

Again they got lucky. Within sight of the Arkansas River they found fresh outlaw tracks. They surprised the outlaws near Garfield and recovered six mules and two horses owned by Vail, and the outlaws' wagon. But the posse's horses were too tired to chase the outlaws, who rode off.

The two groups making up the posse returned with the stolen animals on Sunday, July 26, Colson and his men to Caldwell, Sheriff Davis and his men to Wellington. Vail manager L.T.

Williamson was delighted. He rewarded the 10-man posse $300 to be divided equally among them.[70]

◊

Sheriff Davis had little rest before Caldwell officials telegraphed him asking that he find and arrest the suspected horse thieves. Justice of the Peace James A. Dillar issued warrants for their arrest based on information from Dr. P.J.M. Burkett whose source again was Last Chance proprietor A.C. "Mack" McLean. Davis again organized a posse and left Wellington Monday evening. He arrived at Caldwell at 2 a.m. Tuesday, July 28.

Sheriff Davis hid outside of Caldwell and waited for others to join him. Help soon came from all directions. Caldwell settlers were fed up. They left nothing to chance. Some 150 to 200 joined up with Sheriff Davis and his small posse he brought with him.

Suspected members of the horse thief ring included L. Ben Hasbrouck, William L. "Billy" Brooks, Sewell "Charlie Smith" Ford, Judson H. "Judd" Calkins, Dave Terrill, and A.C. "Mack" McLean himself.

The wife of Caldwell's Presbyterian minister Jacob B. Rideout had occasion to meet up with these men in the past. She described L. Ben Hasbrouck as "a young lawyer, about 22 years of age, and considered the most handsome young man in that country. He had been educated in the city of New York, and not only had more than usual ability as an attorney, but possessed those qualities which are requisite in any young man in order to make him a gentleman of the first class. But he was not a good man. He kept bad company and spent more money than he could honorably earn . . ."[71]

Hasbrouck became Caldwell's first lawyer in 1871. But it wasn't long before neighbors believed he had ties with horse thieves. He spent much of his time in their company and often frequented the Last Chance Saloon. Late in 1872 he was accused of stealing a cow. He defended himself when his case finally came up eight months later.

"The most important case tried at this term of the District Court," said the Belle Plaine paper, "was the State of Kansas vs. L.B. Hasbrouck – a lawyer of Caldwell, in this county, - who was charged with stealing a cow, on or about the 16th day of December 1872, said cow being then and there the property of one Seymore Dye.

"The prosecution was conducted by C. [Charles E.] Willsie, Judge [J. Wade] McDonald and Judge Adams. Mr. Hasbrouck, by himself, W.C. DonCarlos [J.H. Sain?] and Judge Blodgett. The case was well conducted upon both sides by the distinguished counsel in charge, and considerable feeling manifested by both prosecuting witnesses, defense and attorneys. The jury, after hearing the arguments, retired to their room at nine o'clock P.M. on [August] 14th, and at ten o'clock the next day returned into court with their verdict, which read as follows: 'We the jury in this case find that the [defendant] is not guilty'."[72]

This verdict incensed many Caldwell settlers. Later rumors showed what others thought of him. Some settlers latched on to one rumor that reflected their wishes rather than reality. "The report that L.B. Hasbrouck, an attorney at Caldwell, . . . had been lynched by vigilantes proves to be untrue," said the Wellington paper.[73]

William L. "Billy" Brooks, after serving as a lawman in Newton and Ellsworth, drifted to the opposite side of the law. He became a buffalo hunter around Dodge City before switching sides and stealing horses with gangs of thieves. Favorite spots for these thieves were the cattle trail ranches throughout Kansas and down through Indian Territory. These road ranches catered to the wild side.

"He had lived at Caldwell but a short time and was doubtless a bad man," said Mrs. Rideout. "He was very large and about 30 years of age. The day before the arrest he was in town with a rifle looking for another desperado that he might kill him."[74]

Sewell "Charlie Smith" Ford, sometimes known as "One Armed Charlie" kept on the move. (An accident in his past left him with only one arm). He frequented cattle trail ranches and usually could be found somewhere between Wichita and Caldwell, drinking and carrying out business known only to the horse thief gangs.

Ford, according to Mrs. Rideout, had been "very much degraded on a account of strong drink. During the previous winter he sat day after day in front of the saloons dressed in the same old brown suit. His hair was long and matted. He slept wherever night found him . . . He was so completely under the influence of whiskey and so thoroughly controlled by bad men that he would not listen to any words of friendly counsel from those who would gladly have befriended him."[75]

Judson H. "Judd" Calkins owned a livery barn in Caldwell. He too spent time around suspicious characters who left their horses in his barn. George Freeman said Calkins also operated the City Hotel.[76]

Dave P. Terrill had close connections with saloons in Caldwell. John E. "Curly" Marshall sold the Last Chance to him before leaving town in 1872.

A.C. "Mack" McLean, present owner of the Last Chance, came under suspicion because of his close association with the outlaw bands. Burkett may not have yet told others about McLean's role in fingering the outlaw band members.

Sheriff Davis organized his large posse and had them surround the Caldwell area. Then they closed in and systematically rounded up the suspects one by one.

They found Judd Calkins at the City Hotel. Hasbrouck in a cornfield near the Last Chance, A.C. "Mack" McLean at his home near the Last Chance, and Dave Terrill three miles northwest of town at J.L. "Deacon" Jones' house.[77] Sewell "Charlie Smith" Ford ran for his life, riding south into Indian Territory. Some of the posse caught up with him the following day about 25 miles south of Caldwell. None resisted arrest.

They tracked Billy Brooks to his dugout on Fall Creek. Brooks knew he had little chance to escape the vigilante's rope if he gave up. His wife stood by his side ready to defend him. Rev. Jacob B. Rideout's wife told what happened at the dugout.

"When the sheriff and his men rode up, Mr. [Brooks] at first refused to allow himself to be taken," Mrs. Rideout said, "and the following conversation took place.

> Sheriff Davis: Come out and give yourself up like a man.
> Billy Brooks: You'll never take me alive.
> Davis: If you'll give yourself up, I'll defend you from the mob and you'll have a fair trial.
> Brooks: I'll never get to Wellington alive.
> Davis: I have control of my men, and if you give yourself up, I pledge my word you'll have a fair trial.
> Brooks: I know the mob will hang me and I will not give myself up alive. If you take me, you'll take me a dead man. But I'll sell my life as dearly as possible.
> Davis: I'll give you ten minutes to send your wife out of the dugout.
> Brooks: My wife will assist me, so proceed as soon as you like.
> Davis: Send your wife out and we'll let her depart in peace. I do not wish to fight a woman.
> Brooks: My wife will not leave. She is a better warrior than you or any of the men you have in your crowd.
> Davis: You're foolish to lose your own life and endanger the life of your wife rather than defend yourself before an honorable court with the probability of being set at liberty.
> Brooks: I'm not afraid of an honorable court, but I understand mob law too well to expect any such thing as that should I give myself up as a prisoner today. So I shall not throw myself into the hands of a mob, but I do not object to dying here. I have the advantage and will sell my life as dearly as possible.
> Davis: I have 200 men and it will not take long to bring you out.

Brooks: I know that, but you will exchange a good many
   lives for mine. I'm all ready, so go right ahead without
   any more talk.[78]

Mrs. Rideout, whose source probably was Brooks' wife,
described Mrs. Brooks as a small, pale, woman with large eyes and
short curly hair. Rideout said Mrs. Brooks backed her husband all
the way. She begged for him to resist arrest. But an unidentified
friend convinced Brooks to give up and promised he would be safe.
   Sheriff Davis and his posse hauled the prisoners to Wellington,
where Brooks, Hasbrouck, Calkins, and McClean were charged with
theft and with being members of a horse thief band. Sewell Ford
and Dave Terrill were never charged. Terrill was soon released.
Calkins was released on bond. Brooks, Hasbrouck, Ford, and
McLean spent the night (Tuesday, July 28) in the county jail. Next
day, McLean was released after Judge Dillar scheduled his trial for
August 5.
   Caldwell residents became bitter about the release of three of the
six suspects. Pioneer settler, attorney, and later state representative
William Hackney later claimed he and his brother Os had a hand in
getting Calkins and Terrill released.
   Their only crime, according to Hackney, was that they were
caught, "one in his restaurant with feeding bad men and the other, in
his livery stable, feeding bad men's horses. They were friends of
mine, and while we were in favor of helping the whole outfit, Os
Hackney and I decided [vigilantes] should not hang these two men,
and while it looked like we probably would go with them, we were
obdurate and [the vigilantes] did not hang them."[79]
   The next day, Wednesday, July 29, only Brooks, Hasbrouck, and
Ford remained in jail. They hoped their luck held out for another
night before their trial.
   That day Rev. Rideout felt he had to go to Wellington. "My
husband, understanding the storm that was brewing, concluded to
follow the prisoners and befriend them as much as he possibly
could," said Mrs. Rideout. "He said he felt very guilty to think he

had not been more in earnest in seeking the salvation of those poor unfortunate fellows, who had souls to be saved or lost, and he concluded to make another effort to bring them, like the poor one at Jesus' side, within the everlasting arms of love."[80]

When Rev. Rideout reached Wellington at sundown, he went to Sheriff Davis and asked to see the prisoners. Davis said "Not tonight. You may go in the morning."

This did not satisfy Rideout. He made up his mind to go to the jail anyway.

A friend overheard him say he was headed to the jail. The friend asked Rideout to stop at his house first. The friend's wife wanted to talk to him. When Rideout went in the house, the friend locked him in.

Near midnight the prisoners heard men break in. Their worst fears unfolded before their eyes.

That night the moon shone brightly. A light southwest breeze blew. Vigilantes multiplied. By midnight several hundred of these armed horsemen were ready for action.

Soon the only sound that broke the stillness of the night was tramping feet. Vigilantes surrounded the jail, forced the guards to let them remove the prisoners, and marched the three men south to Slate Creek. There the vigilantes lynched the three men.

Later that morning Rev. Rideout walked to the creek. As he crossed the bridge he saw three bodies hanging from the same limb of an oak tree.

L. Ben Hasbrouck "was near the end of the limb, and perhaps 20 feet from the ground," said Mrs. Rideout. "His feet were swaying to and fro and his brown hair, streaming in the wind, occasionally fell over his purple forehead. Next to him was the body of [Sewell "Charlie Smith" Ford] dressed in the same old brown jacket and overalls that he wore the previous winter while sitting in front of the saloons, and near the trunk of the tree was the body of [Billy Brooks] whom the sheriff allowed to fall into the clutches of a drunken mob to be murdered.

"The bodies were taken down and laid in the court house and my husband was standing there as Mrs. [Brooks] came in. She had followed her husband 25 miles on foot and she fell on the floor by his side and wept as though her heart was ready to burst with grief."[81]

◊

Caldwell druggist Dr. P.J.M. Burkett and Burr Mosier, who ran the Buffalo Springs ranch along the Chisholm Trail in Indian Territory, both testified at A.C. "Mack" McLean's trial on August 5. Both told similar stories. Both said McLean had nothing to do with stealing horses or mules. And Burkett admitted McLean played a crucial role in catching the horse thieves. McLean was acquitted.

This horse thief lynching cooled the ardor of horse thieves around Caldwell. For a while the town had little trouble from such outlaw bands. But it continued to suffer.

Farmers struggled for survival in the middle of a drought. And the same day McLean spent time in court (August 5) grasshoppers devoured what was left of the farmers' crops. And settlers feared another Indian raid.

These threats scared off a number of Sumner County inhabitants, who headed back east. Only the hardiest remained.

◊

Two weeks after McLean's trial, on Wednesday, August 19, Caldwell saw more bloodshed. The trouble began when Caldwell shoemaker Frederick Ricer and L.L. Oliver, a 24-year-old who had been in town about a month, drank together in a Caldwell saloon. Ricer himself had been in town only a few months.

Later that day Oliver went to Ricer's shoe shop and saw a pair of boots he liked. The two men bickered about the price, but Ricer wouldn't sell the pair for what Oliver offered. Oliver left peeved. Ricer went back to work repairing boots.

Oliver soon returned, pulled out a pistol, and shot Ricer dead, one bullet hitting him in the neck. Townsmen quickly took Oliver into custody. Had not cooler heads prevailed, they would have lynched him on the spot.

They took Oliver to a cabin where guards watched him. Rev. Rideout happened to be in town that day and heard about the killing. He went to the shoemaker's shop to see for himself. Then he hurried to the cabin to see Oliver. Oliver's hands and feet were tied.

Mrs. Rideout said "My husband asked [Oliver] why he had committed such a dreadful deed. The young man said he did not intend to kill the shoemaker, but only to scare him, and that he was sorry, and asked my husband to pray for him.

"During the first of the evening there was quite a crowd in and around the cabin. . . About 10 o'clock the crowd began to disappear, and by 11 they were all gone except one man, who was left as a guard. Occasionally a man would come and look in at the door. The prisoner begged my husband to remain until morning, feeling confident that the minister's presence would save his life – at least for that night."[82]

By midnight all was quiet. No moon shone. Rideout decided it was time for him to leave.

Shortly after he left, vigilantes entered the cabin and took Oliver. A quarter mile east of town they left him hanging from a cottonwood tree.[83]

"Chisholm Trail can no longer be used..."

Caldwell survived horse thieves, murderers, dishonest land speculators, angry Indians, drought, and grasshoppers, though the cumulative effect in 1874 had dire consequences. "The consequences of these disasters were that both a large proportion of our own settlers and the tide of immigration lost faith in Sumner County," said Andrew A. Richards. "The population of the county was cut down one-half and did not come up to its former figures for two years."[84]

It survived all that. But could it survive a dying cattle drive? The town had its hands full in answering that question for the next few years.

The cattle trade kept Caldwell in business. Town founder Charles H. Stone's vision proved true. Locating where the Chisholm Trail entered Kansas had advantages. The first year saw the greater part of 600,000 head pass by Caldwell. This brought plenty of business. The second year, 1872, brought a large share of the business of 350,000. The third year picked up with 450,000 to 500,000 cattle passing. But 1874 dropped drastically. By then several changes worked against the future of cattle driving, at least along the Chisholm Trail.

Farmers filled the country in ever increasing numbers. They complained about the disease Texas cattle brought and worked toward ending the drive. And they worked toward outlawing all Texas cattle in the state. Farmers despised the image rowdy cowboys brought to the town nearly as much as they feared Texas fever.

Though the death rate in cow towns such as Caldwell may not have skyrocketed, as Robert Dykstra noted, Caldwell's wild and dangerous atmosphere was not entirely a product of 20th century imagination and exaggeration. Those who lived through those days defined Caldwell the same way.

"Caldwell was located on the old Chisholm Trail and has been during all its history a 'cattle town,'" said Richards. "Consequently, it has always had in and about it a class of people who have caused many scenes of disorder and bloodshed, which, if they were chargeable to the county, would not give it a good name by any means. From its location, it has always been a favorite resort of the cow boy and the desperado when off duty and in its earlier days was a decidedly fast and dangerous locality."[85]

On the other hand, Caldwell merchants saw the handwriting on the wall if they didn't retain the cattle trade. They could struggle for other types of business in a dying cattle town along a dying cattle trail or work toward becoming a railhead town where thousands of head of cattle were shipped out.

Town founder Charles Stone may have been the first to face this crisis. He kept track of cattle passing through. Any change directly affected him and all other town businessmen.

"Perhaps the most nearly accurate estimate of the size of the 1874 drive would be one based on a record of the Texas herds that entered Kansas at the dusty town of Caldwell," said Wayne Gard. "There C.H. Stone, a pioneer merchant, kept a list in which he noted each herd and its number of cattle. Up to about the last of July his tally showed a total of 162,127 head. As the trailing season was nearly over and as not a great many herds missed Caldwell, the total drive probably did not much exceed 175,000. That was little more than a third of the half million head for 1873."[86]

So the year 1874 brought crisis to Caldwell that worried merchants and town leaders for good reason. Not only did it look like drovers were dying out and along with them the prospects for a railroad. Indian raids, drought, horse thieves, and the 1873 economic recession only exaggerated the problem.

Between 1874 and 1879 Caldwell faced this challenge to its cattle business with a two-pronged attack. They exaggerated the positive and downplayed the negative while working toward attracting a railroad.

The county newspaper played its part in putting a positive spin on Caldwell's problems. It reflected an approach common to the frontier presses of that day. "To succeed, an editor had to be optimistic and believe that his town was destined to become an important and influential place in the West," said David Dary.[87]

On the positive side, Caldwell residents could point to encouraging agriculture statistics. Farmland in Sumner County rapidly spread after 1874. For example, while that year saw some 4,800 acres planted in winter or spring wheat, the next year, 1875, saw the wheat crop more that tripled with 15,280 acres planted. By 1878, the figure exceeded 83,000 acres.[88]

Between 1875 and 1880 Sumner County as a whole saw rapid growth in settlers, as did the entire state. "By 1875 all public land in Kansas had been surveyed," said historian William Zornow. "Each year from 1875 to 1879 the amount of public land disposed of to settlers increased approximately 100,000 acres until in 1880 the annual distribution reached the two million mark."[89]

Settlers could also argue that horse thief activity nearly ceased after 1874, at least for a time. Saloons still drew customers, but cowboys were scarcer. Locals felt Caldwell had settled down.

A gradual change in the cattle business took place through the 70s. An increasing number of cattlemen settled around Caldwell, raising a meatier, tamer breed locally rather than trailing longhorns from Texas. This didn't completely replace the trail herds, but it did give Caldwell part of its business.

For the next five years the hottest topic in town centered on a railroad. "The railroad fever is prevailing here at this time to an alarming extent," said the Caldwell Items section of the Wellington paper. "From what I can learn I conclude that a proposition to aid any line of road that will make Caldwell a point can be carried in this township by a large majority."[90]

Actually railroad talk had started when the town began. Railroad proposals came and went. In July and August 1873 Caldwell hoped the St. Joseph, Kansas, and Texas would put tracks from Oxford through Wellington and to Caldwell but the deal fell through.

In late 1874 and early 1875 Wellington businessmen tried to raise interest in the Texas, Wellington, and Northeastern Railroad which would go through Caldwell and Wellington before heading to Kansas City and east. The local paper summarized the need in Caldwell.

"But all of these points within the state are settling up so rapidly that the range is cut off – besides the large amount of damages that the cattle men are compelled to pay for the destruction of crops – renders them unprofitable points for shipment and therefore the necessity of a railroad to the line of the Indian Territory where the cattle men can hold large herds of cattle without being subjected to large damages and can ship at will. We find that from Caldwell over the Texas, Wellington, and Northeastern Railroad, Kansas City can be reached in less number of miles than from Wichita over the Atchison, Topeka, and Santa Fe."[91]

Again the deal fell through because the promoters couldn't raise enough money. This became a recurring problem. Meanwhile farmers continued to oppose the cattle trail business. And occasionally the farmers seemed justified.

"A quarrel between a party of Texas cattle men and the citizens of Caldwell Tuesday [April 27] resulted in a fight, the Texans opening the ball by firing several shots from their revolvers," said the paper. "The fire was returned by the citizens and a brisk fusillade was kept up until the Texans retreated. Citizens then mounted and a running fight was kept up until the Texans were captured. One of the party afterward escaped by mounting a fleet horse and riding away followed by a shower of bullets, none of which however took effect. The others were magnanimously released upon a promise to leave the city in double-quick time."[92]

Clearly funding a railroad continued to be a hard sell while business in Caldwell diminished. Farmers opposed anything that encouraged the presence of cowboys. Even some townspeople had trouble with the high price tag asked by railroad companies. But by the end of the 1875 trail driving season it became obvious that most herds would turn west and head for Dodge City or other western locations.

Merchants saw the only real chance for success as coming from railroad business. The grassland just south of town provided a perfect range for fattening cattle. This cattle market was just waiting for such a railroad.

The newspaper continued to play its role. "Letters are received almost every day from persons in eastern states asking what lots on Main street can be bought for and if there is any vacant business houses to rent," it said. "Also what land can be purchased for in the vicinity of Caldwell, all of which goes to show that Caldwell will be the city of Southwestern Kansas."[93]

In the middle and late 1870s, Kansas began filling up with settlers. With these increasing numbers came increasing crops. Between 1875 and 1880 winter wheat land increased from a half million to 2.2 million acres. Overall cultivated land in Kansas grew during this period from 4.7 to 8.8 million acres.[94]

Statistics in Sumner County reflected what had been going on through the second half of the 1870s. The county rated as one of the top five Kansas counties in growing winter wheat, producing nearly one and a half million bushels by 1882. That year it also led the state in number of animals slaughtered or sold for slaughter.[95]

This meant the Caldwell vicinity in the late 1870s was becoming increasingly crowded with farmers and their crops while still serving as a cattle center near the Cherokee Outlet even before a railroad passed through town. And in fact both types of business could use a railroad to haul their product. But if a railroad never located in Caldwell, merchants believed they would miss out on lucrative sources of income. So they continued to work every angle to attract one.

A glancing survey through the town paper for the rest of the year and into 1876 shows how it tried to draw more traffic. Sometimes subtle, sometimes outright, sometimes appealing to business, sometimes to culture, the 1876 *Caldwell Post* tried whatever it could to bring more people to the town.

"L.P. Williamson, of Vail & Co.'s stage line, was in this place last week looking after business. He is going to stock up the route in good order with four horses to each coach instead of two as it is at present." (May 27)

"Our streets are crowded with teams every day and our merchants are having a lively trade. Mr. C.H. Stone was in town last week. He is holding his cattle about ten miles south of here." (June 10)

"Last fall Messrs. Gastic and Baker, living near this town, bought 100 head of cattle for $1,200 and sold them a few days ago for $3,000 and still some men think there is no money in handling cattle." (June 17)

"A large number of cattlemen are making Caldwell their headquarters. C.H. Stone sold 170 head of two-year-old steers last week at $15 per head." (June 24)

"Plenty of Texas men in town and Caldwell presents an appearance as in former years when from three to ten thousand head passed through every day.

"A herd of Texas cattle passed through town last Sunday numbering 3,800 head in charge of F.D. Norton and owned by Messrs. Woodland, Osha, and Speed of Frio City, Frio County, Texas." (July 1)

"Caldwell has one advantage over most of towns, and that is, it never gets so dull so that we can get up a horse race or a dance." (July 22)

"Notwithstanding the withdrawal of the cattle drive, Caldwell is far from a dead town and local trade is fairly active." (August 12)

"Mr. B.F. Buzard of St. Joseph, Mo. was in town last week. He has located on Bluff Creek west of here, is fixing up a ranch, and is going into the cattle business on a large scale." (August 26)

"Five miles northwest of Caldwell, at the Dixon School House, they have a district school of 35 scholars and also a Sabbath School and preaching every Sunday. Miss Maggie Harrington teaches the district school, N[oah] J. Dixon is superintendent of the Sabbath school, and Rev. J.B. Rideout holds services every Sunday at 10 a.m." (September 9)

"Hank Zuber has purchased a team, turned granger, and is at present engaged in turning over the soil and preparing to sow wheat. We predict he will make a first-class granger." (Sept 16)

"The trail is literally lined with teams all the while hauling freight to different points in the Territory. Why don't [sic] the A.T.& S. Fe R.R. Co. extend their line to Caldwell?"

"At least three hundred thousand pounds of freight passed town [on] the trail last week." (October 21)

"We are sorry to lose Mr. [Andrew] Drumm from our midst. He has taken his cattle to Medicine Lodge to winter them. Like Daniel Boone, this country is getting too thickly settled for him, as he had neighbors within about four miles of him." (October 28)

"Many of our farmers are paying ten to fifteen cents per bushel for hauling wheat to Wichita; and we have conversed with many of them that are in favor of doing anything reasonable in order to get a railroad to Caldwell. They think that what they pay now to get their wheat to market would pay their tax on railroad bonds for a good many years. Then let's have a railroad, and if we can't get a broad gage, get a narrow gage." (December 2)

"Two miles from Caldwell (our little village of about one hundred inhabitants) are several quarter sections of the very best kind of land, which can be preempted at $1.25 per acre, paid in one year after filing. We have in our little town a good schoolhouse, a church organization of 25 members, and our citizens are very kind accommodating people. There is some vacant land at a distance of a mile from our schoolhouse, where we have an excellent school.

"Caldwell has been a very rough place on account of its being located on the great Texas cattle trail, but at the present time I think it will compare favorably with any other town of the same size in the west." (March 30, 1876)

But all the positive press you could get didn't change the fact the trail through Sumner County was closing. Once that happened, Caldwell had nothing to replace that lost business.

The legal end to the Chisholm Trail seemed to sound Caldwell's death knell for its Texas cattle business if nothing changed. In March 1876 the paper announced the trail's end.

"The famous Chisholm Cattle Trail, which passes through this country from south to north ten miles west of Wellington, and which is the finest natural road in America, can no longer be used as a 'Texas Cattle Trail.' By a recent legislative enactment the Texas cattle quarantine grounds have been removed to and beyond the west line of Sumner County."[96]

Some of the local merchants still tried to profit from the cattle trail business. Caldwell saloonkeeper Hank Zuber figured he could go to the customers if they didn't come to him. A Caldwell correspondent for the Wellington paper went along with him.

"A few days ago we took deck passage on Hank Zuber's prairie schooner," the correspondent said, "which was loaded with flour, bacon and beans for Mr. Hood's hungry cowboys on the trail about 14 miles west of this place where he is holding about 10,000 head of cattle."[97] No doubt Zuber also had a supply of liquid refreshments.

Merchants suffered more from the drop in cattle trail business than did farmers. An increasing number of farmers continued to move there to work the area's rich soil.

Meanwhile cattlemen favored the lush grasses in the Cherokee Strip and the Cherokee Outlet just south of Caldwell. Increasing numbers drove cattle north, then stopped south of town to allow their herds to fatten up before driving them further west or east. By August 1876 settlers jumped the gun in trying to buy land in the Cherokee Strip, which was soon to become Kansas land.

"Settlers on the strip lands who are desirous of filing on their claims are advised to remain patient until the Register at Wichita is authorized to receive filings," the paper advised.[98]

By early 1877 cattlemen got their wish. They could move cattle to the Strip and buy the land with few restrictions. A Wichita paper explained some of the details.

"That fine tract of land, averaging about two and a half miles in width, lying on the southern border of Kansas, known as the Cherokee strip, is now in the market," it said. "It is open to actual settlers only, for one year from the 7th of this month. Direct entry can be made upon any of these lands included between range 8 east and 10 west at the U.S. Land Office on Douglas Avenue in this city [Wichita].

"However, we notice the requirements are different in settling on this strip from [what is] necessary upon the Osage Trust Lands. A settler has only to make affidavit to the effect that he is an actual settler upon the land he desires to purchase, also the date and amount of his improvements, and that there has been no prior settlement made by any one upon said tract. No specified time of residence is required.

"At the expiration of one year from the 7th of February 1878, all lands remaining unsettled will be sold under direction of the Secretary of the Interior, to the highest bidder in tracts not exceeding 160 acres to each purchaser, and at not less than one dollar an acre."[99]

This proved to be a precursor to cattlemen moving more permanently into the Cherokee Outlet. Until a railroad came to Caldwell, cattlemen would divert their herds west to Dodge City or other towns with tracks east.

On May 7, 1877 more talk started up about another railroad. It led to a proposal for the Kansas City, Emporia, and Southern to run from Oxford to Wellington and down to Caldwell financed by bonds not to exceed $4,000 per mile. Shortly after that came another proposal for a narrow gauge, the Solomon, Arkansas Valley, and Eastern, which would involve the same expense. Before a special election took place July 2, townspeople became more animated.

"Frequent public meetings were held in every school district," said John Edwards. "Even the children discussed the railroad problem. In the midst of this tumult the officers of the L[eavenworth], L[awrence], and G[alveston] railroad system gave notice that they would extend their railroad into this county in the near future. The election of July 2nd resulted in a majority of 173 for the K[ansas City], E[mporia], and S[outhern] proposition and a majority of 207 for the S[olomon], A[rkansas] V[alley] and E[mporia] proposition. There the whole matter has rested."

People continued to talk about the railroad propositions but nothing more happened. In the meantime the town held out hope and merchants found ways to increase business. Hank Zuber opened a new saloon in a recently built 18 x 40 foot structure.[100]

Frustration over no railroad periodically surfaced. "As our citizens are very anxious for a railroad, we hope this county will soon have a good square business proposition from the [Atchison, Topeka, and Santa Fe Rail Road Company]," said the paper.[101]

Tension mounted as citizens noticed town leader Charles Stone leave town to seek business elsewhere. "Mr. C.H. Stone and family moved to Wichita last week," said the *Press*. "Mr. Stone was one of the founders of this town and was engaged in the mercantile business here for several years."[102]

The same issue of the paper announced "The stock dealers formed an association at Caldwell, Saturday, [November] 24th. Enos Blair was elected President; F.A. Hunt, Vice President; J.R. Musgrove, Secretary; and Sim Donaldson, Treasurer. An executive committee consisting of Messrs. J.W. Hamilton, Charles Hatfield, and B.W. Hall was appointed."

Countering the loss of Stone, the paper continued its positive approach. "Caldwell, 26 miles southwest of Wellington, is a thriving town with a population of 300 and undoubtedly will be the terminus of the Southern branch of the A.T.& S.F. railroad." (February 28, 1878)

The June 13 issue of the *Sumner County Press* ran a more detailed summary of Caldwell. It argued that even without a railroad the town could prosper.

"In company with Capt. L.K. Myers we drove to Caldwell, 25 miles southwest, last Friday, arriving in time for a late dinner at the Caldwell House. We had not visited the town for nearly three years and of course the changes noted in the features of the country were surprising. At that time that portion of the county was sparsely settled and farming had only been indulged as an experiment. The Indian scare, the grasshoppers and drought of 1874 had almost depopulated the southern border and the transfer of the cattle trade to points further west had left the village with but a precarious trade and little hope for the future.

"The year 1875 brought but little change for the better. But during that year a few early settlers had succeeded in getting their lands into such a state of cultivation as to prove the wonderful capacity of the soil for the production of the staple grains. This added to the natural beauty and attractiveness of the fertile bottoms and undulating table lands invited an immigration that, beginning with the autumn of 1876, has since dotted the country all over with residences and other improvements. Miles of wheat fields, each surrounding the unpretentious structure made to answer temporarily the purpose of a residence for the owner and his family, stretch away to the north and west, mingling with the green of the prairies and forming a picture of exceeding beauty and interest.

"The population of the country has quadrupled since our former visit and still the immigration pours in. The village itself has recovered from its torpor and enjoys an active and increasing trade. Several new business houses and a large number of residences have been added since the halcyon days of Texas cattle traffic and stocks of general merchandise have been substituted for the 'First and Last Chance,' where festive cowboys were wont to imbibe the liquid hell, warranted to discharge a navy revolver at half cock.

"The town is now well supplied with lines of staple good and enjoys an excellent trade. Messrs. Dixon and Houghton and G.G.

Godfrey have good stocks of dry goods and general merchandise.
J.H. Sain has a neat stock of drugs and notions and runs the post
office in connection therewith. Mr. F.G. Hussen has recently
opened a hardware store and tin shop and does a good business.
Hoss and Kelly and two or three other firms deal in groceries and
provisions. Hank Zuber has one of the finest rooms in the county,
tastefully arranged for a billiard hall and saloon. J.M. Thomas
dispenses justice and deals in real estate. Two hotels accommodate
the traveling public. The Caldwell House, J.H. Wendels, proprietor,
retains its original popularity and daily grows in grace with its
guests.

"A steam saw and grist mill supplies lumber and corn meal to the
settlers. The machinery for manufacturing flour is to be added in
time to begin work on the new crop of wheat.

"This portion of the county is well watered and weeded and the
land for agricultural and grazing purposes is first class. Settlers
have all the advantages of schools and church organizations and
government lands may yet be secured in sight of immense grain
fields." (June 13, 1878).

Not to shortchange cattlemen, the *Press* said "A large number of
cattle dealers are making their headquarters at this place." (July 11,
1878). Soon cattlemen would have a better reason for staying.

Two months later more talk about tracks to Caldwell surfaced.
On September 17 Major W.H. Schofield and Major O.B. Gunn,
representing the Kansas City, Burlington, and Southwestern
railroad, offered to build from Oxford to Wellington at $4,000 per
mile. Shortly after this Ross Burns, representing the Atchison,
Topeka, and Santa Fe, offered to build from the northeast corner of
Sumner County through Belle Plaine, Wellington, and on to
Caldwell. These two companies fought each other, both trying to
offer a better deal than the other.

By November, the Santa Fe had the upper hand. The *Press*
frequently mentioned the Santa Fe proposition.

"By last Saturday's mail, Capt. L.K. Myers of this city
[Wellington] received a proposition from the Atchison, Topeka &

Santa Fe Railroad Company offering to extend the Wichita branch of that road into and across Sumner County," it said. "The Company agrees to enter the county at or near the northeast corner of the county and build by way of Belle Plaine and Wellington to Caldwell. The points involved in the proposition are as follows: The road to be completed and operated to Wellington, September 30th, 1879 – next September. To be completed and operated to Caldwell, December 31st, 1880." (November 7)

"Hon. J. Mulvane, of Topeka, in response to the earnest solicitation of a few friends of the A.T.& S. Fe R.R., was present and gave us a plain, concise and satisfactory statement of the condition, intentions and future prospects of the company. ...We now have our first proposition from the company." (November 21).

Citizens held a special election on December 31 to decide which railroad should build tracks through Sumner County. The Santa Fe won out. The bond issue carried by a vote of 1706 to 1041. The county issued bonds not to exceed $4,000 per mile or $180,000 total for not more than 45 miles of track.[103]

Santa Fe exceeded its promise. The Cowley, Sumner, and Fort Smith tracks reached Caldwell on May 31, 1880. It included 37.8 miles of track between Mulvane and Caldwell. The first train came to Caldwell on June 13.[104]

Once people knew a railroad would reach Caldwell, the town grew by leaps and bounds. While the town hovered around several hundred at most through the 70s, by 1880 the federal census counted 1,979 people living in Caldwell Township, which included Caldwell.[105] And by the middle of the next decade it numbered in the thousands. The railroad to Caldwell became a landmark event, changing the town from a small, dying trail town to a flourishing railhead cattle-shipping center. Had it not been for competition from another railroad built simultaneously to Hunnewell, Caldwell would likely have become the leading Kansas cattle town of the early 80s.[106] As it was, it became a cattle town second only to Dodge City.

Caldwell's new status brought not only new business, but also new problems common to all cattle towns. In fact, Caldwell's problems with law officers exceeded any previous town.

"Caldwell will be the metropolis of the southwest."

Changes in Caldwell preceded the railroad's arrival. People knew Caldwell would soon change from a trail town to a cattle-shipping center. After clinching the deal for a new railroad early in 1879, the town bustled with excitement and hope.

It attracted major cattlemen and more business. Cowboys filled the town while the trail herds they led fattened up to the south. Indians came to town frequently to buy and trade. New businesses, including saloons and bawdy houses, drew a wilder crowd.

New buildings went up a block west of old Chisholm Street. Many of these were made from brick or stone in contrast to the early log structures. It took little time for Caldwell to go from a trail town of a couple hundred residents to a trade center with close to 2,000.

Historian Bill O'Neal listed a variety of businesses that flourished in the 80s. They included saloons: Fitzgerald's, the Occidental, the Red Front, Moore Brothers, the Golden Wedding, Moreland House, the Kentucky, Phillips', the Exchange, Robison's, Flatt and Horseman's, the IXL, the M & S, and the Red Light.

They included a variety of stores, such as A.S. Groh's Cheap Cash Chicago Store, the Lone Star Clothing House, H.A. Ross & Co. Dry Goods, Horner's Drug Store, W.N. Hubble & Co. General Merchandise, Hulbert's Gun Shop, Hockaday's Tinware and Hardware, Levi Thrailkill's, Smith & Ross' Grocery Store, Charles H. Fay's Grocery, the Morris Grocery, and York-Parker-Draper Co. Besides that there were hotels, an opera house, two banks, three churches, a school, livery stables, restaurants, lumberyards, jewelry stores, a bookshop, tonsorial parlors, and a Chinese laundry.[107]

In 1879 town leaders, while optimistic about Caldwell's future, knew more business meant more trouble if they weren't careful. Up till then the town had not been incorporated.

Township constables or the county sheriff along with posses and sometimes deputy U.S. marshals handled lawbreakers. The town had no need for a city government as long as there were only a handful of settlers. But as Caldwell grew to over a thousand residents, leaders knew they had to incorporate.

Before town leaders had a chance to organize a city government, gunshots rudely introduced this new era. A July 1879 incident gave a foretaste of what was to come.

On Monday, July 7, 1879, two cowboys stirred up trouble near Caldwell's Occidental Saloon. George Wood and Jack Adams, who worked for Johnny Nicholson in driving a herd from the Chickasaw Nation, arrived in Caldwell around 6 p.m.

They headed straight to the Occidental for refreshments. Then they went outside where a band was playing. According the Wellington paper they "began firing at blazing turpentine balls which some boys were tossing into the air." The Caldwell paper said the two cowboys were "egged on by one H.F. Harris, a sneak-thief ruffian."

Citizens complained to township lawmen. Wood and Adams returned to the Occidental for more drinks. Soon Constable W.C.B. "Wash" Kelly, Deputy Constable John Wilson and six posse members, including 27-year-old George W. Flatt, arrived on the scene.[108]

The lawmen waited for a while hoping Wood and Adams would come back outside. Then Wilson and Flatt entered.

John Wilson, who had worked as a sign painter, paperhanger, and as an Occidental Saloon employee, led a short and troubled life, according to historian Richard Lane. Several years later he came to a violent end.[109]

George Flatt's past before Caldwell remained a secret. George Freeman said he was "formerly from Texas and, like most of the Texans who visited Caldwell, was a lover of strong drink and a frequent visitor of the Red Light."[110] The previous February he bought the Occidental from James M. Moreland, though Moreland returned to running it a few months later.[111]

Wilson walked to the back of the room. Flatt followed but stopped at the bar in front. Wood and Adams drank nearby.

Flatt laid his six shooters on the bar and called for a drink. Finishing, he grabbed his guns and readied for action. The Caldwell paper said Wood and Adams cocked their guns. The Wellington paper said Wood and Adams "made a menacing movement toward Flatt."

"[Flatt] backed toward the door only two or three paces... Reaching the door first, Flatt stepped to the sidewalk and to the south side of the door," said the Wellington paper. "Wood and Adams... reached the door and [Adams] sprang to the sidewalk when the firing began. Adams received a fatal wound... Wood received two desperate wounds and staggered toward the inner door where he met Wilson who fired on him. Wood fell to the floor. . . Wilson upon leaving the saloon was fired on by [W.H.] Kiser, one of the posse, and slightly wounded. . ."

The Caldwell paper said Wood and Adams, after cocking their guns, headed for the front door. Flatt backed toward the front door ahead of them.

"On reaching the door, [Wood and Adams] leveled their six shooters on [Flatt] demanding his arms. Flatt replied, 'I'll die first.'

"And at that instant one of the fellows fired, the ball passing close by Flatt's head and grazed the temple of W.H. Kiser... Flat then drew both his pistols which he had kept concealed behind him and fired with the one in his right hand at the man who had got farthest out the door [Adams]... which caused [Adams] to drop heavily to the sidewalk and rolling off in the street died almost instantly.

"The man who stood in the door and shot first [Wood] received a ball in the right side which passed straight through his body from the pistol held in Flatt's left hand. The man returned the fire at Flatt, and then turned and fired at Wilson, who was closing in the rear. The ball grazed Wilson's wrist... Wilson returned the fire so rapidly that the man failed to get his work in... Wilson's first shot took effect in the right hand ... and the second in the abdomen ... from which [Wood] fell, shooting Wilson in the thigh as he went down."[112]

George Freeman, who witnessed the event, said Flatt panicked afterwards. He ran out in the street and emptied his guns by firing at the sidewalk.[113]

Two inquests took place. Coroner James M. Thomas conducted the first shortly after the event. A jury of six people heard the evidence into the next morning. Sumner County Coroner John H. Folks conducted the second two days after the incident. Both concluded the lawmen were justified in killing the cowboys.

This shootout turned George Flatt into a town hero. He was still riding high in his hero role three weeks later when District Court Judge William P. Campbell ordered Caldwell incorporated on Tuesday, July 22. The town elected a city council and Noah J. Dixon as mayor on Tuesday, August 7.

The mayor and city council then passed ordinances. The third one, adopted on August 14 and published in the *Caldwell Post* on August 21, allowed for the mayor to appoint a city marshal. Dixon chose Flatt. The ordinance also left the choice of deputy marshal and other assistants to the marshal. Flatt chose Daniel William "Red Bill" Jones.

◊

Deputy Jones, age 33, had many friends in Caldwell. His experience as a lawman dated back to 1872 when he served as a township constable in Wellington, Kansas.[114] The following year he became Wellington city marshal.[115] He took his job seriously, though he still had a few wild oats to sow.[116]

Sometime in the middle 1870s, Jones moved from Wellington to Arkansas City. And after that he moved to the Red Fork Ranch in Indian Territory to manage it. During all this time he also worked as a deputy U.S. marshal. Between his job overseeing the Red Fork and serving as a deputy marshal, he had little time to relax although he did when he could.

As a deputy U.S. marshal, Jones often chased outlaws throughout southern Kansas. In February 1874 he went from Arkansas City, Kansas to Wellington and reported to the *Sumner County Press* about his experience hunting for horse thief Henry Miles.[117]

When Caldwell druggist J.H. Sain took a trip to Fort Sill, Indian Territory in 1875, he visited the ranch. "Reached Lee & Reynolds' old ranch at noon," he said, "and found Dan Jones, an old Wellingtonian, in charge."[118]

Jones continued to stay in touch with Wellington friends for a while. "Dan Jones, formerly of this place [Wellington], but now keeping a ranch on Red Fork, I.T., was in town several days last week, shaking hands with old friends."[119]

Jones often had occasion to head up the trail to Caldwell to buy supplies and visit new friends. He became a well-known figure in Caldwell. "D.W. Jones, of Red Fork, I.T., who has been stopping in [Caldwell] for several days, returned to his ranch last Sunday," said J.H. Sain. "Dan was among the earliest settlers of this county and a firm friend to Wellington during the struggle for county seat."[120]

In the fall of 1876, Jones continued his role as deputy U.S. marshal when he investigated the murder of Richard Wannamaker, a middle-aged German. Wannamaker was traveling from Medicine Lodge, Kansas through Indian Territory on his way to Texas when someone blasted him with a shotgun.

The murder took place several miles northwest of Red Fork ranch. "Dan Jones, the keeper of the Red Fork Ranch, some seven or eight miles down Turkey Creek, was the recognized leader among the scattered inhabitants of white men in this portion of the country," said Sam Ridings. So Jones rode north to investigate. Two Indians he met said they saw a dead man north of there. The Indians led the way to the body.

"Just as we descended into the bottom, after a ride of four miles, the sun was setting," Jones said. "A cold wind from the northwest blew in our faces and the tall waving grass made spectres [sic] of the long shadows that fell across our path as we sped along the stream.

"We passed down a steep bank into the timber and I found myself in the midst of an Indian camp where everything was in confusion. At a word from my guides, they all uttered something . . . unintelligible to me, but quiet was restored.

"My guide, dismounting, signaled to me to do the same, saying, 'Come.' Then on foot I followed the Indian who went stooping and dodging through the brush some four hundred yards, when he halted and pointed ahead, said, 'See,' and in the growing darkness I beheld the body of the dead man. Upon approaching the body I found it to be of a man about fifty years of age.

"He was lying on his back, his right arm across his breast, his left arm thrown out. He had been shot with a shotgun, the charge entering the left side of the face and many of them coming out on the right side of the ear. The left pocket in his pants was wrong side out, showing that he had been searched."

Soldiers from Fort Sill tracked down the killer. They caught up with him in Jacksboro, Texas.[121]

Often some Caldwell citizens visited Jones at the Red Fork ranch. "A party left [Caldwell] last Thursday morning [Dec 14] for Dan Jones Ranche on Red Fork, I.T. in quest of turkeys."[122]

Jones enjoyed their company. And many in Caldwell enjoyed Jones' visits. They even stretched rules to allow him to join a Caldwell club when he asked. Bachelor Jones joined Caldwell's Gooseberries Club in March 1877. The club consisted of bachelors over 30. "The Gooseberries will stretch their rules just enough to admit Dan Jones into the club," said J.H. Sain.[123]

Jones stayed busy as a lawman. "Mr. D.W. Jones returned from Ft. Smith last Saturday [October 6, 1877] where he has been in attendance at the U.S. District Court as a witness against John Robinson who shot Pat Canon at Red Fork, I.T. last July."[124]

His success as a lawman and a Chisholm Trail ranch owner still left him hoping to hook up with a partner of the opposite sex. He never gave up trying.

"D.W. Jones, of Red Fork Ranche, I.T., has sent us a fine view of his ranche which shows that Dan has got his things fixed up in fine style, and from the number of teams and groups of men standing around, and the Pan Handle stage leaving the ranche with horses on the keen run, shows it to be a place of considerable importance and we would think Dan would never get lonesome.... Dan tells us to show the view of the ranche to the girls and if any one wishes the position of Mrs. D.W. & C., to send her along. He proposes to pay all charges."[125]

On December 31, 1878 near tragedy struck. That Tuesday morning Jones rode away from the ranch to tend to a herd of cattle. On the way his horse tripped and threw him. The fall broke Jones' leg.

He couldn't stand up enough to get back on. He was too far from civilization to get anyone's attention. He could think of only one thing to do. He strapped up his broken leg and started crawling toward a ridge he knew overlooked the Red Fork ranch.

Jones crawled all day and through the night. Next morning he spotted the ridge. He crawled all that morning and into the afternoon before he reached it. Once at the top, he waved his hat.

George Haines, who was at the ranch, thought he saw a hunter waving at him. Haines went to the man and was surprised to see it was Jones. By then it was three p.m. Haines took Jones to the ranch and got a doctor to take care of him."[126]

Why Mayor Dixon chose George Flatt rather than Dan Jones to be marshal came down to the July 7 shootout. Dixon may have felt pressure from the town. Many there still indulged in hero worship.

Had the choice come down to the best lawman, no doubt Jones
would have been the man.

Yet Jones may not have wanted the job anyway. He could
collect his salary from Caldwell with less responsibility and
continue work as deputy U.S. marshal.

◊

The longer Flatt received top billing as marshal, the more he
alienated others. He seemed to attract foes like flies.

Back in February George Flatt bought the Occidental Saloon
from Jim Moreland.[127] But by July Moreland again managed it.
When the July 7 shootout ended, Flatt accused Moreland of giving
one of the cowboys a pistol. Flatt smashed open the front door of
the saloon with a chair and pistol whipped Moreland.[128]

Less than two weeks after the July 7 shootout Flatt opened
another saloon with partner William Horseman, who would replace
Flatt as marshal.[129] Soon they were at loggerheads.

The first recorded arrest in Caldwell's new era as an
incorporated city had nothing to do with cowboy antics. On
September 6, 1879 Flatt arrested J.H. Wendels for "fast driving."
He pled guilty and paid a $3 fine.

One month into serving as city marshal, on Tuesday, September
16, George Flatt hitched up with 17-year-old Fannie Lamb. The
wedding took place "at the residence of H.A. Todd on the Pole Cat
[Creek] although . . . it was quite an enjoyable affair, being attended
by a goodly number of the elite of the city."[130]

Among these "elite" were Mayor Noah Dixon and Deputy
Marshal Dan Jones and his wife. Jones was married in 1879
sometime before Flatt since he and his wife attended Flatt's
wedding. The *Caldwell Post* mentioned a marriage between "Mr.
William Jones" and Bertha Fossett on Friday, September 11, five
days before Flatt married Fannie Lamb.[131] This was a different
Jones.

Guests at Flatt's wedding gave gifts. Dixon gave the couple a lamp. The Joneses gave Mrs. Flatt a necklace.

A week later, on Tuesday, September 23, 1879, Mayor Dixon died suddenly.[132] Five weeks later, on Tuesday, October 28, the town chose St. James hotel clerk Cash Hollister, who ran against W.N. Hubbell, as the new mayor. Hollister preferred not to run for re-election. He remained on the job till next election on April 6, 1880, when former Wichita city marshal Mike Meagher became mayor.

Gunshots sounded in the streets of Caldwell on Wednesday, October 29, 1879, the day after Hollister became mayor. They first came from cowboy John Dean when Marshal Flatt and Deputy Marshal Dan W. "Red Bill" Jones asked Dean to give up his firearms to comply with the city ordinance. Dean "mounted his horse and started out of town firing his revolver promiscuously. . . At the crack of his pistol the marshal and deputy turned loose with their six shooters." No shots found the mark, but Dean was arrested the same day. He pled guilty and paid a fine.[133]

On Saturday, November 22, Marshal Flatt arrested Mayor Hollister for assaulting J. Frank Hunt. Hollister paid a $2 fine. Two days later Hunt was arrested and fined for assaulting Mayor Hollister.[134]

Caldwell businessmen meanwhile looked forward with special relish to the coming cattle drives. They finally had a railroad to ship cattle, at least in the near future. They exuded optimism like no other time. They sent circulars to Indian Territory and Red River Station inviting Texas cattlemen to head their way. They believed they could steal the cattle business from Dodge City.[135]

Caldwell predicted boom years for the foreseeable future. Hope filled the streets and hit a new high.

Commenting on plans for a new opera house in town to be financed by Col. Stobaugh of Fort Reno, Indian Territory, the *Post* boasted, "Caldwell will undoubtedly be the metropolis of the southwest – she has the surrounding country to back her up, besides being the shipping point for military and Indian supplies, and is the main trading point for the territory and northwest Texas. When Maj. [D.M.] Odum, one among the largest cattle dealers of the state of Texas risks $8,000 in a hotel as he has here, we may not hesitate to remark that Caldwell's future is a foregone conclusion."[136]

No other shootouts happened for the rest of Marshal Flatt's term. But by the next election on April 6, 1880, the shine wore off Flatt's popularity. His hero worshippers were few and far between. Mostly citizens hoped to move on to more reliable peace officers. Flatt seemed to like drinking more than marshaling.

On Monday, April 12, new mayor Mike Meagher chose William N. Horseman to replace George Flatt. Dan Jones continued as assistant marshal and James Johnson became a policeman. Shortly before the election Dan Jones' wife gave birth to their first son. The first week of May, Meagher appointed J. Frank Hunt as a deputy policeman.

Meagher came to Caldwell in 1879 after distinguishing himself as an outstanding Wichita city marshal. He served from April 1871 till April 1874. He became a deputy U.S. marshal in 1874 and in June became a lieutenant in a militia company protecting Kansas' southern border. In April 1875 he again became Wichita city marshal and stayed in that position till April 1877.

He arrested a number of cowboys during his time as city marshal and avoided gunplay till New Year's Eve, 1876 (New Year's Day, 1877). That night Sylvester Powell tried to shoot him while he was inside an outhouse. Powell sent two bullets through the outhouse, one going through Meagher's coat and the other through his leg before Meagher burst out, gun blazing. Meagher chased Powell and ended up shooting him through the chest, killing him instantly.

Meagher moved to Caldwell after seeing Wichita settle down from being a cow town to a farm community. By the late 1870s Wichita lost its cattle trade to Dodge City and other towns to the west.

George Flatt increasingly frequented his favorite saloons and, contrary to a Caldwell city ordinance, continued to wear a gun. His excuse: he claimed to fear for his life from enemies he had made

"Caldwell will be the metropolis of the southwest."

while marshal.[137] Also he still worked as a detective. Caldwell law officers now looked at him with a combination of fear and hate.

"Caldwell outdid Dodge City."

Citizens expressed confidence in their new mayor, Mike Meagher. They liked his choices for law officers. They believed William Horseman would make an efficient city marshal. They knew Dan Jones had backbone. And they thought James Johnson and Frank Hunt would work out well as policemen.

These lawmen seemed ready to deal with cowboys and cattlemen arriving with the 1880 trail drives throughout the next few months. The Cowley, Sumner, and Fort Smith Railroad completed tracks to Caldwell in June. It looked like this would be a boom year for Caldwell.

"It soon became a certainty that Caldwell would be a shipping point for a large amount of cattle – some coming through from Texas, and others held in the Territory and surrounding country – and that the railroad company contemplated to build extensive cattle yards here," said the paper. "This fact becoming generally known soon resulted in a large addition to our population."[138]

Furious construction projects filled the town. Businessmen desperately scurried about trying to complete work before the expected boom. April saw a number of changes.

A new paper, the *Caldwell Commercial*, began publication. Horner got a new soda fountain. Street graders worked away. A stone building at the southern part of town neared completion.

Horse teams headed to Wellington for lumber to build Andy Spear's opera house. George and Mag Wood[s] tore down their building in Wichita and brought some of the material to Caldwell to construct the Red Light Saloon.

Doubleday Brothers began construction of a furniture store on Main Street. Newt Moore began building stores on the north side of the Kentucky Saloon. Cozine & Collins and R. Rue started up kilns to make bricks.

Boyd & Anderson were about to start a meat market east of the Kentucky Saloon. Wilkin Brothers, from Emporia, were about to open an ice cream and confectionery store.[139]

The cattle season lasted from the middle of April to the middle of October. During that time Caldwell became as wild as Dodge City. Town leaders welcomed the increased revenue while hoping to stem gunplay. Most of the money came from the prostitution, liquor, and gambling, according to court records.

Fines from 188 arrests totaled $833. Court costs added several times that income. Prostitution counted for 62 arrests and $390. Besides that the city collected $44 from prostitutes arrested 15 times for drunkenness and disturbing the peace and five more arrests were likely related to prostitutes for another $30. That meant $464 – more than half the total income – came from prostitution.[140]

Liquor arrests came in second. Counting the 15 prostitutes arrested, 53 arrests totaling $101 in fines came from drunkenness and disturbing the peace. Gambling arrests came to 31 and took in $149.[141]

Lawmen had their work cut out for them. Outbursts of exuberance meant business for them. For example, on Saturday night, April 24, 1880 a soldier armed with a six-shooter got rambunctious. He broke out windowpanes and vowed to take out any lawman who tried to stop him.

When Dan Jones and James Johnson found out, they "gathered him in and gave him quarters in the cooler. Afterwards a sergeant came and paid the soldier's fine and took him to camp where he was drilled in the old fashioned, but very disagreeable, manual of 'right shoulder and left shoulder log'."[142]

On Tuesday evening, May 11, a soldier and a gambler argued over a Keno game at one of Caldwell's saloons. Soon fighting broke out, soldiers against townsmen. Marshal Horseman "got a

94

whack along the side of the head. Dan Jones had his foot stepped on, judging from the way he tripped around. For a while it was lively, as the number of cut heads and bloody noses bear witness. The cooler received its portion of the spoils of the row."[143]

The town hoped to prevent such incidents but found the task next to impossible. They didn't want to discourage cowboys from spending their money. The town tried to walk a fine line.

"The problem for the cattle town people," said historian Robert Dykstra, "was not to rid themselves of visitors prone to violence, but to suppress the violence while retaining the visitor."[144]

On Thursday, June 3, 1880, policeman James Johnson nearly met his maker. At midnight T.J. Ingraham, contrary to a city ordinance, carried a pistol. When Johnson asked if he had a revolver, Ingraham said, "Yes, you son-of-a-bitch." He pulled it out, put it to Johnson's head and pulled the trigger three times.

The gun misfired. Johnson grabbed the pistol and fought it from Ingraham, then arrested him. Ingraham was fined $10 and court costs, then released.[145]

◊

Wednesday, June 16, 1880 saw the first cattle herd loaded on the new railroad and shipped east. It marked the beginning of the new era for Caldwell – from trail town to cattle shipping trade center. On Tuesday evening, June 22, telegraph wire connected Caldwell to the rest of the country, "thus giving us lightning communication with the commercial world," said the local paper.[146]

Excited talk filled the streets. Some Kansas City and Chicago cattle buyers came to town. Even Joseph G. McCoy came. Leading drovers headed to this new railhead. C.C. "Lum" Slaughter trailed 1,000 head there. So did others, such as John Dawson (1,900) and W.H. Murchison (3,400).[147]

As luck would have it, almost immediately Caldwell saw stiff competition from Hunnewell, about 12 miles east of town and a half-mile north of Indian Territory. A branch of the Kansas City,

Lawrence, and Southern Kansas railroad, called the Sumner County railroad, built tracks south from Wellington to Hunnewell and the town was ready for shipments the same day Caldwell shipped its first herd. Hunnewell prospered for the next 13 years.[148]

' But even with that competition, Caldwell boomed. In one way it outdid Dodge City.

"The new market at Caldwell . . . took some business from Dodge City and outdid it in cattle shipping for the season," said Wayne Gard. "While Dodge City shipped 17,957 head, a slight drop from 1879, Caldwell loaded 25,531 head. Dodge City, which drew from both trails, received many more cattle than Caldwell – 287,000 head by the end of August – but most of the herds were trailed on to Nebraska or beyond."[149]

Mayor Meagher and city lawmen knew they had their hands full. Excitement filled the streets. Businessmen eagerly welcomed the cattle business. Cowboys celebrated in their usual way – frequenting saloons and bawdy houses.

◊

Lawmen needed all the help they could get. Having George Flatt in town flaunting his freedom to carry a holstered gun among cowboys who were forced to go unarmed didn't help. "Flatt was not afraid of the officers, and he knew the entire police force were afraid to arrest him."[150]

Three days after that first cattle shipment headed out of Caldwell on the new railroad, George Flatt reaped the whirlwind from the ill will he had sown. His waterloo came early Saturday morning, June 19. All day and late night Friday led up to that fateful Saturday. That weekend Flatt went on a bender. He saloon hopped, from dance hall to the Kentucky Saloon, to the I.X.L. Saloon, before his companions convinced him to stop.

Though Flatt alienated most people, he still had a few friends. Early Saturday morning he left the I.X.L. Saloon and headed south down the east side of Main Street with two companions; Charles L. Spear and Samuel H. Rogers.

Spear, to his left and closest to the buildings, walked a step ahead of Flatt while Samuel H. Rogers, who had served as Flatt's deputy and was still on the police force, walked to Flatt's right and a step behind him. Flatt carried two guns.

Rogers described that evening. He said he "went with Flatt and the others from the dance hall to the Kentucky Saloon, and then went over to the I.X.L. Saloon. Flatt was accustomed to sleep in rear of that saloon. [I] tried to get Flatt to bed, [but Flatt] said, 'I want to go and take a lunch first'."[151]

So Flatt headed south to Louis Segerman's Restaurant. It was around one a.m. Spear and Rogers knew that the previous night Flatt tangled with lawmen Frank Hunt and James Johnson. Flatt pulled a gun on both of them and threatened to shoot Johnson's feet off. And before that Flatt had challenged Marshal Horseman's authority. Spear and Rogers feared retaliation and hoped to remove Flatt from that danger.

As the three men walked south, the inebriated Flatt bragged, "I'm the cock of the walk here." Seconds later a shotgun blast shattered the evening's stillness. Sparks fell around Flatt's head. More shots followed, perhaps a dozen. The first shot came from the north behind the three men. Rogers said the blast nearly deafened him in his left ear. Other shots came from across the street.

The first blast from the north sent buckshot through the base of Flatt's skull, under his left shoulder, and several other places. Flatt fell forward on his right side and rolled over on his back, head facing the southwest. He died instantly.

"Let up. You've killed that man," Rogers called out to the unknown gunmen. Within a minute the entire police force appeared on the scene. All carried firearms, though only Dan Jones held a long-barreled weapon.

Chaos reigned for a time. As excitement abated, town leaders tried to sort out the chronology of the evening's events. Later that morning County Coroner John H. Folks arrived on the train from

Wellington. He held an inquest to get at the facts of the killing. Dr. William A. Noble and Dr. D. MacMillan examined the body.

The coroner and a jury met across the street at Meagher & Shea's Saloon to find out what happened. The two doctors discussed the fatal wounds. After lunch, Sam Rogers told what he saw. The inquest broke up for the day. Flatt's funeral and burial took place that afternoon. The inquest continued on Monday, June 21.

Monday afternoon Charles Spear told what he knew. The doctors explained more about the wounds. Policeman James Johnson and jeweler H.A. Ross filled in what they could. After that the inquest closed its doors to the public.

The men behind the assassination remained a mystery. Four days after the killing, Flatt's wife gave birth to a boy.

The next day, Friday, June 25, Sheriff Joseph Thralls came to Caldwell with several deputies. He arrested Mayor Mike Meagher, City Marshal William Horseman, and policemen Frank Hunt, James Johnson, Dan Jones, George W. McFarland, and R.H. Collins. Thralls also took in Hugh A. Ross, Dr. D. MacMillan, Dan Rogers, Charles Spear, and William Thompson. That afternoon they headed back to Wellington on the train.[152]

The hearing took place Monday through Wednesday (June 28 through June 30). The judge released all except Horseman and Hunt. That same day the Caldwell city council fired the police force. Meantime the justice of the peace in Wellington immediately issued warrants to re-arrest all the men except Collins.

Caldwell appointed replacements. They included City Marshal C.F. Betts; Deputy Marshal John Rowen [Rowan]; and Policeman John Wilson.[153]

Mike Meagher's case came up the second time. This time Wellington Justice of the Peace I.N. King conducted the hearing on Saturday, July 3rd. The court soon released Meagher, but Horseman, Hunt, Jones, and Johnson were held over for the next term of district court. The court set the bail at $500 each. The judge later ruled them not guilty. On July 8 Caldwell rehired their original police force.

The public remained in the dark about the case. Evidence never saw the light of day as to why Sheriff Thralls arrested Caldwell's entire police force. Some accused Wellington leaders of arresting Caldwell's police for monetary reasons. "It looks not only like a money making scheme, but also a scheme to cast odium upon the city of Caldwell," said one Caldwell paper.[154]

Common sense did point to the police force, since they were first on the scene and carried weapons. People in Caldwell didn't seem to care a whole lot one way or another. Their greatest concern, or at least that of the merchants, came down to business. With Flatt's conflict with police a thing of the past, merchants and cattlemen could pay more attention to business. After all, Texas cattle herds filled the town. Caldwell was still in its peak period. Most hoped to "strike while the iron was hot."

With Flatt's disruptive influence gone, people got back to business with a vengeance. Few showed concern over George Flatt's death. Most thought he had it coming. Even the conspiratorial nature of his murder aroused little interest.

But Marshal Horseman couldn't seem to stay out of trouble. Sheriff Joe Thralls arrested him and Frank Hunt on Thursday, July 15 for "assault and battery on the person of Abram Rhodes."[155] Though the court later discharged Horseman and Hunt, the Caldwell city council decided they needed a change. They fired Horseman on Tuesday, August 10, and hired James Johnson to replace him. The council also reappointed Hunt and hired Newt Miller as a policemen.[156]

As business in town settled down in the coming fall and winter off-season, citizens saw a bright future. Caldwell now successfully competed with the busiest cow town in existence. The future definitely looked bright. Businessmen were jubilant.

"Without any visible assets…"

The lively cattle business came to a standstill by the end of summer, 1880. Most townspeople figured lawless behavior would also die out since the cowboy traffic slowed down. At the same time the town hoped business those cowboys brought would continue and increase the following season. How to have one without the other continued to be a balancing act.

Thursday afternoon, September 2, 1880, a cowboy named W.F. Smith spent some time in the Red Light before feeling his oats. He began shooting his revolver. When police arrived at the scene, Smith mounted his horse and rode off. Word spread Smith was wanted by the law in Hunnewell as well. Police spread around the city in search of the wanted man.

Policeman Frank Hunt found Smith at a livery stable. When Hunt ordered Smith to give up, Smith drew his gun. Hunt sent a shotgun blast Smith's way. Buckshot caught Smith in the knee and killed his horse. "A great deal of sympathy was expressed for the horse," said the paper. Smith pled guilty to disorderly conduct, paid his fine, and Dr. William A. Noble treated his wound.[157]

Caldwell hoped to leave its Wild West image behind. But events kept preventing it. At least the next one held off till after the busiest part of cattle season. It happened about four months after Flatt's death. It involved Frank Hunt.

Caldwell followed the practice of other cow towns with seasonal business. They reduced their police force in the off-season to save money. Ever since October 4 Marshal James Johnson, who had replaced William Horseman on August 10, worked as the lone town lawman, the fourth town marshal if counting the brief term of C.F. Betts. Some felt this created a dangerous situation.

"Some of these odd days – or nights – the City Council will awake to the realizing sense that one policeman is too small a force for the preservation of order in a town the size of Caldwell," said one editor.[158] Even he was surprised at how soon his words proved true.

Trouble seemed to center around dance halls. Troubles there usually had to do with women. Saloons mostly attracted men who liked to drink, play cards, and gamble. Dance halls drew men looking for women. Prostitution thrived. The most popular dance hall in Caldwell in that first cattle season was the Red Light.[159]

Former Policeman Frank Hunt, one of the casualties of Caldwell's trimmed down police force, frequented the Red Light. He had left the force only a few days when he found himself a target at the Red Light on Friday night, October 8. According to the *Caldwell Commercial*, he got in a disagreement with a woman and her man before he sat down at the north window of the dance hall.[160]

Shortly after 10 p.m., a shot rang out. Hunt jumped up and yelled, "I'm killed!" Pointing out the window, he said "He did it out there." Hunt fell to the floor.

City Marshal James Johnson and Special Policeman Dan Jones ran to the east door, which was locked. Jones returned to the front door and headed out after the shooter. Johnson forced the east door open and ran to the north side. He heard running footsteps, but the shooter escaped.

Friends laid Frank Hunt on a table where Dr. D. MacMillan examined him. The bullet had entered Hunt's left side near the back. Several men carried Hunt to the Leland Hotel. There he remained in pain for the next two days. His brother came from Missouri to be with him. On Monday, October 11, around noon Frank Hunt died.

Both Dr. William A. Noble and Dr. D. MacMillan examined the body more thoroughly. They said the ball that killed Hunt "passed through the upper portion of the tenth rib, through the liver and the lower part of the stomach, and lodged to the right of the stomach."[161]

Between the time Hunt was shot and died, he fingered the killer. The coroner's inquest concluded that David Spear shot Hunt and that a man named Lumis or Loomis was an accessory.[162]

Shortly after Hunt's death, the police arrested 17-year-old David Spear, son of Charles L. Spear. (Charles was with George Flatt at his assassination. David's older brother, George W., later became embroiled in the Mike Meagher shootout).[163] Dave Spear had been in the Occidental Saloon when the George Flatt murder occurred back in July 1879.

Sheriff Joe Thralls chased down and arrested the other suspect, Loomis, in Wellington. The Caldwell papers never mentioned what happened to Loomis after his capture.

The October 28 issue of the *Post* said "The prosecution of David Spear, charged with the murder of Frank Hunt, was concluded last Friday [October 22], the defendant being released."

Caldwell's city council reacted to pressure from citizens to beef up the force. On Monday night, November 1, it added men. "Joe Dolan was appointed assistant," said the *Post*, "and one Reed was appointed special policeman at the Red Light. Mr. Reed is under full control of the city and marshal but is paid by Mr. [George] Wood[s] at whose request he was appointed."[164]

Ironically, after this first season of cattle drives heading to Caldwell to be shipped by rail, and with Caldwell's saloon liquor sales growing, prohibition became state law. The disjuncture could not have been more extreme.

On November 2, 1880 Kansans voted on a state constitutional amendment. The amendment said, "The manufacture and sale of intoxicating liquors shall be forever prohibited in this State, except for medical, scientific and mechanical purposes.

Prohibitionists won the vote. Sumner County ranked in the top five prohibition counties, voting two to one in favor of the amendment.[165] Likely the most prohibition votes came from Wellington and Belle Plaine rather than Caldwell.

Governor John P. St. John knew this amendment needed teeth. Specific details about what constituted a breech of the law and penalties attached became the next step. On February 19, 1881, St. John signed the Alfred Washburn Benson bill which did just that. The bill went into effect on May 1, 1881.[166] That meant the 1881 cattle season in Caldwell as well as Dodge City would take place with prohibition in full force as state law.

◊

On Wednesday, March 16, 1881, Sheriff Joe Thralls arrested James M. Moreland in Caldwell for "highway robbery" committed a year earlier. Moreland was well known to Caldwell residents.

He had sold the Occidental Saloon to George Flatt back in 1879 before taking back control prior to Flatt's July 1879 shootout. Moreland's brother Patten "Pap" Moreland, ran Caldwell's popular Moreland House. Texas cowboys knew Pap's wife as "Mother Moreland" and liked her home cooking.[167]

A year earlier Jim Moreland along with Count Roberts and Dick Baker planned and carried out a scheme to rob a man named McGraw. A Wellington paper recounted the details.

McGraw came from Michigan to Wichita with $1,000 to invest in real estate. In Wichita he ran into Count Roberts who talked him into going to Marion Center to meet two others, Dick Baker and Jim Moreland. Roberts said they would take him on a free tour to see what was available. McGraw believed him.

Roberts took McGraw to Jim Moreland's house in Marion Center where McGraw met Moreland and Baker. Right away the three men tried to convince McGraw to give his money to them to invest, but McGraw refused and asked to see what was available.

Roberts hitched up a wagon and the two headed out to view the land. After riding about 20 miles, McGraw watched, horrified, as two masked men on horseback rode up with pistols blazing.

Roberts jumped out of the wagon while the two masked men robbed McGraw. When the robbers rode off, McGraw headed east.

He traveled northeast till he found work as a farm hand in Burlingame, Kansas.

There he told fellow workers of his bad luck at Marion. Word spread. Jim Moreland and Dick Baker heard about it. They kidnapped McGraw at gunpoint and forced him to sign an affidavit exonerating them. McGraw gave up on the west and headed back to Michigan.

McGraw's friends didn't give up. They hired a Topeka detective named Cole to track down the culprits. Cole's efforts paid off. Count Roberts was captured in Wichita; Dick Baker in New Mexico; and Sheriff Thralls found Jim Moreland in Caldwell.[168]

◊

The second year of Caldwell's new status as a railhead brought more business. It became the peak cattle season for the town. It also brought turmoil in the city council over who should serve as marshal. That year, 1881, saw no less than five marshals come and go. That year also brought a bank failure and financial ruin to a number of its citizens.

During this boisterous and busiest of all cattle seasons Caldwell took on the title of "Border Queen." According to historian Richard L. Lane, one could trace the title back to a June 1881 issue of a newspaper in Indian Territory called the *Cheyenne Transporter*. That same month a Caldwell merchant began selling Queen of the Border cigars.[169]

Though the 1881 cattle season started slow because of a bad winter, herds again took the Chisholm Trail to Caldwell. Fewer herds passed by and more stopped and left on Caldwell trains. Caldwell loaded 31,644 while Dodge City loaded 33,564.[170]

On April 4, 1881 W.N. Hubbell replaced Mike Meagher as Caldwell mayor. Hubbell chose John W. Phillips as the town's fifth marshal, replacing James Johnson. Hubbell also appointed Newt Miller as deputy marshal.

But a month later the city council decided to reduce the marshal's salary from $60 to $50 a month. Phillips said he would quit if they insisted on the salary reduction. The council upheld their decision. They accepted Phillips' resignation on June 29.

This came at a bad time. Cattlemen and cowboys filled the streets during the peak season. On July 18 Mayor Hubbell nominated John Brown for marshal. The council rejected Brown. Hubbell nominated Mike Meagher. The council rejected him. On July 27 Hubbell appointed Meagher as a temporary replacement till they could find a permanent marshal.

Five days later, on August 1, Mayor Hubbell nominated Meagher and James Roberts as candidates for permanent marshal. The city council decided on Roberts.[171] In September Mayor Hubbell resigned as mayor because of opposition he kept facing from several councilmen over his choices for marshal. Cass Burrus replaced him. James Roberts quit as Caldwell's seventh marshal. John Rowan replaced him.[172]

In spite of the new prohibition law, Caldwell's Red Light owner George B. Woods heard opportunity knock after the 1880 cattle season. Hunnewell now had a huge new hotel to board drovers and cattlemen during the busy season. This confirmed Woods' belief in a new market. Increased cattle traffic meant increased drinking. To him, Hunnewell begged for another saloon. In the spring of 1881 he opened one. He even provided transportation between Caldwell and Hunnewell to encourage business.[173] And business there thrived.

The Red Light Dance Hall and Saloon in Caldwell continued to prosper as the 1881 season picked up. Late that summer it again became the center of attention.

On Thursday night, August 18, 1881, around 8 p.m. Red Light owner George Woods tried to keep a lid on some domestic violence at his dance hall. One of his employees, 21-year-old Lizzie Roberts, was having trouble with a patron, Charlie Davis.

The two had lived together for some time before Lizzie Roberts left him five weeks back and began to work for Wood[s] at the Red

Light. Charlie Davis, from Texas, wanted her to leave the Red Light and go live with him again. She said no.

That's when George Woods came between them. He told Davis to leave. Davis, three feet away from Woods, pulled out a "Colt improved 45" and shot him a few inches above the navel. The bullet went through Woods and into a partition behind him.

Woods jumped on Davis and the two fought their way out the front door. Davis escaped and ran uptown where he surrendered to a policeman. Woods staggered back in the house and to the back door before falling on the floor.

He told his wife to "catch Charlie Davis and prosecute him to the full extent of the law." Then Woods died. Davis escaped from the police and wasn't caught till 1883.[174]

George Spear later managed the Red Light. Mag Wood[s] still owned it.[175]

◊

Caldwell's city council under Mayor Cass Burrus continued to have trouble finding a permanent marshal. Toward the end of October they desperately searched for someone to replace John Rowan.

Mayor Burrus and the council asked Meagher again to fill in. Meagher refused. They asked George Brown and Dan Jones. They both refused. They finally got John Wilson to accept.[176]

Bank Robs People

Trouble sometimes came from unexpected places. Few people anticipated bank problems in a growing and prosperous place such as Caldwell. That's why it hit with such force when it did happen. Nothing hit as hard as betrayed trust.

Saloonkeepers were not alone in seeing new opportunities with the growing cattle shipping business. So did bankers. The first banker in Caldwell, J.S. Danford, held an exalted position among

Caldwell residents. He owned the Merchants and Drovers Bank in town, which did a booming business. Danford soon noticed another market at the neighboring town of Hunnewell. He followed Red Light Saloon owner George Woods' example and expanded into Hunnewell with another bank.

Danford's new bank in Hunnewell proved to be successful from the start. This augmented Danford's already high position among Caldwell citizens. Danford's banks looked like the most secure place anyone could keep their money.

J.S. Danford owned a bank in Osage City south of Topeka before starting the ones in Caldwell and in Hunnewell. He knew respected figures of his day, including leading politicians and businessmen.

The Merchants and Drovers Bank in Caldwell served as the preeminent business in town. Danford's background showed success through the years.

Danford said he came to Kansas in 1869 with $1,000 and worked in real estate at El Dorado. He profited in several other businesses before settling on banking. He started the Osage bank first and ran it for three years without a profit. He also ran the Harvey County Savings Bank and sold it for $10,000 profit before starting the Merchants and Drovers Bank in Caldwell. His experience lending money to Texas cattlemen at El Dorado aided him in running the Caldwell bank. Besides expanding in Hunnewell he helped organize a bank in Carbondale.[177]

"He was a man of pleasing address, pleasing manners, and constantly increasing popularity," said journalist Tom A. McNeal. "At one time he enjoyed the reputation of being the most popular banker in the state."[178]

In November 1881 ominous signs surfaced. Rumors spread that the bank was short of funds. Most people refused to believe it. In the last two years, their confidence in Danford had steadily grown. Newspapers recorded this growth.

The January 8, 1880 issue of the *Caldwell Post* described the bank as "organized under the state law of Kansas with double liabilities of stockholders with a capital of $50,000. . . J.S. Danford is president, E.L. Harrington, vice president, and J.R. Nyce, cashier. Mr. Danford is also president of the Osage City Bank and vice president of the Harvey County Savings Bank and is one of the successful operators in Colorado mining stocks. This company also owns over 5,000 acres of land in this county adjoining Indian Territory and within a short distance of this city. This is a much needed institution and the people of this section give it their hearty support."

The February 12, 1880 *Post* said "Mr. J.S. Danford, president of the Merchants and Drovers Bank, was in the city the first of the week looking for a location on which to erect another large building, as the one occupied by them is not as large as their business demands."

The April 1, 1880 *Post* said "The business of the Merchants and Drovers Bank has increased so rapidly that the bank has been obliged to put on more force, and have engaged the services of Byron Bowers, of Wellington, Kansas and J.H. Willis, of Newark, Ohio as bookkeepers."

The June 24, 1880 *Post* announced that the Merchants and Drovers Bank would occupy its new building on Monday, June 28. The bank would use the first two floors of the 23 x 70 foot building while the Masonic Lodge and others would rent the top floor. The bank would even have daily stock market reports delivered by telegraph.

"It is unnecessary for us to say anything commendatory of the bank's president, Mr. J.S. Danford," the paper added, "as he is too well known among our citizens and the cattlemen to require any introduction."

The September 30, 1880 *Post* mentioned that Danford was in town the 28th and 29th. It went on to say "The Merchants and Drovers Bank at this place is a staunch and trusty institution. Its capital is abundant and Maj. Danford and subordinates are men both capable and faithful to their trust. The branch institution at Hunnewell can claim the same advantages. The business men both here and at Hunnewell have the utmost confidence in these banking establishments and well they may."

The November 11, 1880 *Post* said that Danford had completed arrangements "to commence the erection of his stone block on the corner and adjoining the Merchants and Drovers Bank on the north. This block will be composed of two large rooms on the first floor with a city hall on the second floor. This, when completed, will be by great odds the finest structure in the city or southwest, and as the right man has taken hold of it, we can safely say that it will without doubt be constructed."

Danford's success continued into 1881. So people in and around Caldwell found it almost inconceivable to think anything negative about the bank. That's when reality threw a curve.

On Monday, November 21, 1881, several drafts on New York came back protested. These bank customers asked cashier W.D.C. Smith what was going on. Smith said the bank had only a temporary shortage. He said the drafts would be honored if sent to the bank where they were drawn.

People wanted to believe him. Some even deposited money hoping to help with the bank's shortage. Each day that week Smith reassured depositors. He swore they would get their money. Each day he promised the next train would bring $5,000 to $20,000 in currency. But it didn't happen.

On Saturday, November 26, cashier Smith stayed at the bank till three p.m. receiving deposits. He then went to the train station where he met Fred Denman from Osage City and the two left for Wellington. There they met Danford. Danford deeded the Caldwell bank building to cattleman Major Calvin Hood.

"Smith and Danford left Wellington in a private conveyance Sunday morning [November 27], and drove to Wichita, where a telegram was sent by Sheriff [Joe] Thrall[s] to have them arrested on a warrant sworn out by I. B. Gilmore, who happened to be in Wellington and learned of the flight," said the Caldwell paper.

"The sheriff of Sedgwick County [H.R. Watt] started to Winfield Sunday evening [November 27] with the prisoners to have their

preliminary [hearing] tried before [Thirteenth Judicial District]
Judge [E.S.] Torrance, but telegraphed Thrall[s] to meet him at
Mulvane. The party from [Caldwell] got to Mulvane before the
Thrall[s] party arrived, but a telegraphic warrant had been served
upon them [Danford and Smith] before the Caldwell officers
arrived.

"The party came to Wellington where they were met by a
delegation of creditors from [Caldwell]. Talks were had but nothing
could be got out of Danford. They were arraigned before Squire
[I.N.] King, and $50,000 bonds required of them for their
appearance on the Gilmore warrant, which they claimed they would
give on Tuesday [November 29].

"On the afternoon train a delegation of nearly one hundred
arrived, repudiated the action of the first party, and demanded that
the prisoners be taken back to Caldwell or the full amount of the
deposits paid at once. The depositors were not satisfied, and
[Constable Abraham Rhoades] and posse proceeded to gather in the
sheriff [Joe Thralls] and prisoners [Danford and Smith]. A special
train was secured from Wichita, which arrived about 12 o'clock
Monday night [November 28], on which the prisoners were brought
to [Caldwell]."[179]

The *Caldwell Post* story failed to name the "delegation of
creditors" for what they were: a vigilante committee bent on
lynching Danford and Smith. The mob threatened to hang Danford
if he didn't come up with a way to pay back what he owed them.
But Danford proved to be more than equal to the challenge.

The *Post* story failed to include another detail. When Danford
realized what the "delegation" had in mind, he figured he and Smith
would never make it from Wellington to Caldwell alive if he didn't
do something. He quickly offered to hire a special train to take the
entire party to Caldwell rather than have them ride horse back. The
vigilantes bought into the offer.

The vigilantes lived to regret that. But for the time being they
hoped Danford would come up with a way of paying off his debts.

The creditors/ vigilantes held a meeting on Tuesday morning, November 29. They appointed a committee and adopted a resolution which said:

WHEREAS, The Merchants and Drovers Bank of Caldwell, Kansas, has suspended without any visible assets whatever wherewith to pay the claims of its creditors; and,

WHEREAS, The said creditors, having met to consider the ways and means to secure their claims against said bank and its officers.

Resolved, That it is the sense of this meeting that all the securities and moneys of said bank have been fraudulently appropriated and made way with by its president, J. S. Danford, and by his direction and connivance.

Resolved, That the said creditors demand a full and complete showing of the status of said bank, and full and complete settlement and liquidation of all their several claims; and that if immediate payment cannot be made, that the said creditors be secured by ample securities, and that immediately.

Resolved, That we hold each and all the officers of said bank strictly accountable for their acts and deeds in the management of said bank, and that they be prosecuted to the full extent of the law for any violation of their said duties.

Resolved, That we declare it our firm determination to make use of all lawful means to *make* said J. S. Danford settle and liquidate his liabilities caused by his fraudulent practices in the management of said Merchants and Drovers' Bank.

Resolved, That, if deemed necessary, the following attorneys be retained by the creditors of said bank for the prosecution of all claims and demands of these creditors against the Merchants and Drovers' Bank and its several officers, namely: Mr. Thomas George and Mr. Quigley, of Wellington, and Mr. L. M. Lange, of Caldwell, and that a committee be appointed to raise funds for the carrying into execution the

resolution, and that a *pro rata* assessment be made on all
creditors for that purpose. And, finally,

    Resolved, That we demand that the prisoners, J. S. Danford
and W. D. C. Smith, President and Secretary of said Merchants
and Drovers' Bank, be immediately turned over and delivered to
Constable [Abraham] Rhodes [Rhoades], who first legally
arrested the said J. S. Danford and W. D. C. Smith, by virtue of a
warrant issued by J. D. Kelly, Esq., of Caldwell, Kansas, and that
said Rhodes [Rhoades] keep the said prisoners in his custody
until they are disposed of in due form.

    WM. CRIMBLE. Chairman of Committee[180]

Danford said he didn't know the assets of his bank. He said
Smith and Denman took the securities so they could be divided
equally among his banks.

Danford offered to give creditors a personal $56,000 note
secured by $32,500 in Merchants and Drovers Bank notes, the bank
building worth $10,000, a half section adjoining the city worth
$2,000, all his own and the bank's real estate in the county, and
offered to pay any balance personally.

Creditors accepted the offer. Another committee went to
Wichita next morning, November 30, to confirm what Danford
said.[181]

The Merchants and Drovers Bank failure became the most
discussed and publicized event of 1881. J.S. Danford went from
one the most admired men in the area to the butt of jokes. Residents
hated him and still wanted to hang him. But Danford had more
tricks up his sleeve.

Danford explained away the bank failure. He claimed that six
months before the failure he had decided to sell the Sumner County
banks so he could concentrate on the Osage City bank.

He said the Sumner County banks normally had a balance over
$50,000 with the Chase National Bank of New York. But when he
tried to get money from them to cover the run on the Sumner

County banks this time, the bank directors told him they had stopped giving loans in the West.

And Danford blamed a former employee as the culprit who started the run. He said a vengeful former cashier wanted to start his own bank and invented the story so he could put Danford out of business.

All this bought him more time. The Arkansas City paper printed a December 5 dispatch on the matter. "Danford and his creditors made a settlement by which Danford turns over assets amounting to $74,433 to cover his liabilities of $59,666; and S. S. Richmond, of Caldwell, was appointed trustee under bond of $80,000," it said. "Danford and party are now rejoicing in sweet liberty. The town is now quiet and depositors feeling better, though not sanguine of a full payment. Danford and committee of creditors are now en route to Newton to complete the transfers and assignments. All proceedings are to be dismissed upon the completion of the transfers."[182]

Danford returned to his bank in Osage, Kansas to get his affairs together. But while creditors kept waiting to receive the money Danford owed them, Danford had another idea. A Winfield paper said "Danford has sued several citizens of Caldwell for $90,000 damages for carrying him by force to Caldwell, keeping him in durance [captivity] and torture there for several days in which his life was threatened. We suppose he has a good case in law and will probably recover some damages."[183]

Shortly after that the Arkansas City paper said "A few days ago S. S. Richmond, one of the leaders of the Danford mob at Caldwell, went to Osage City on business connected with the wrecked bank. Danford at once served upon him the necessary papers in a suit for $100,000 damages." And the paper went into more detail, sounding more sympathetic to Danford than to those he owed.

"Danford has been arranging and fixing matters for the past three or four weeks," it said, "and from the following from Osage City we presume his labor will result in 'a time' for some of his Caldwell friends who participated in the mob festival.

"S. S. Richmond, one of the principal leaders of the Caldwell-Danford mob, who was appointed trustee of the assets of the Merchants and Drovers Bank, of Caldwell, with powers to settle up the business, came to confer with Danford in regard to some unfinished business. A suit was at once instituted by Danford against members of the Caldwell mob for $100,000 damages, and the papers were served upon Richmond by the Sheriff of this county.

"This takes the case to that county, and enables Danford to have papers served upon other members of the mob in Sumner County and compel them to go to that county for trial. There will be over fifty defendants."[184]

Caldwell creditors tried to possess Danford's property but Danford got the attachments discharged.[185] The Hunnewell city counsel passed resolutions declaring $16,000 worth of Danford's bonds illegal. The counsel also resolved to put a notice in the *New York Herald* warning others about the bonds.[186]

Legal maneuvering between Danford and creditors continued through the following months. Creditors tried to have Danford's bookkeeper W.D.C. Smith extradited back to Caldwell when he was arrested in Fort Worth, Texas, for grand larceny, but they hit a roadblock with Governor John St. John.[187]

In May, the *Winfield Courier* announced that Danford's lawsuit against the vigilantes would result in a trial at the next session.[188] But in September, the two parties agreed to settle.

"On the authority of the attorneys in the difficulty arising between J. S. Danford and his Caldwell creditors," said the Caldwell paper, "it gives us pleasure to state that everything has been amicably settled, and that every creditor will shortly receive his proportion of the amount due him from the M. & D. Bank.

"The basis of compromise, as we understand it, is that Danford agrees to pay 40 cents on the dollar, to withdraw any and all suits against the creditors, and to pay his own costs and expenses. The creditors on their part [are] to release all attachments, turn over all property, books, and papers belonging to the M. & D. Bank, and to dismiss all suits with prejudice.

"A few other small matters remain to be arranged, which will be done within the next three or four days, after which the proper parties will be ready to disburse the pro rata amount to those holding claims against Mr. Danford growing out of the failure of the M. & D. Bank.

"We are assured that, contrary to the belief which has prevailed in this community, Mr. Danford has been making every exertion to secure the means whereby to pay his creditors, or at least offer them something in satisfaction of the amounts they had lost by the failure of the bank. And it is only within the past few weeks that he has been able to make any arrangement whereby he could offer even 40 cents on the dollar.

"He has no money of his own and was powerless to raise any by reason of his property being tied up with attachments and in law suits growing out of his failure. And it is only through friends who have the utmost confidence in his integrity and business capacity, that he is now able to pay even the 40 cents and free himself from the burden which has hung upon him like a dead weight for nearly a year.

"During the first few months following the failure of the M. & D. Bank, the *Commercial* published many things against J. S. Danford, under the impression, from the developments at that time, that his failure was a move merely made to swindle his creditors. However that may have been, now that he has made the best restitution in his power, we are glad that the cloud has been removed from his character in a measure, and trust that he may yet be able to satisfy all parties that no wrong was intended on his part, and that he may in time fully recover the ground he lost by reason of his misfortunes."[189]

Some may have thought this put an end to the matter, but it didn't. W.D.C. Smith, still in Fort Worth, Texas, held up the agreement by refusing to withdraw his lawsuit against the vigilantes.[190]

While this battle continued, J.S. Danford added another hitch. In November, the Caldwell paper, quoting from the *Osage Free Press*, said "Mr. J. S. Danford is very seriously ill and it is impossible to tell when he will be better. His present condition is the result of a concentration of causes, starting with the terrible shock to his nervous system by the brutal mob at Caldwell, and going through more than a year of anxious business work, culminating in the disappointment of a business trip to Denver, and terminating in complete cerebral exhaustion and paralysis of the brain.

"Seventeen days ago he was brought home from Denver in a state of dementia, from which there has been very little improvement. Dr. Eastman of the State Insane Asylum, has been here in consultation with his family physician and agrees with him that there is little promise of speedy recovery, but that with faithful care there will probably be recuperation and restoration to mental and physical vigor. This statement is made by the authority of his physician, Dr. W. L. Schenck, of this city [Osage].

"In regard to Mr. Danford's business matters, we know nothing tangible. Prior to his trip to Colorado, after a long and patient effort, his Caldwell affairs were on the eve of settlement, and would have undoubtedly been settled only for a new and unforeseen difficulty.

"One of the stipulations of the settlement on the part of the Caldwell creditors was that the suits of both Danford and his cashier, W. D. C. Smith, now of Fort Worth, Texas, for damages, should be dismissed. Mr. Smith, it is said, demanded $7,000. This, the Caldwell people nor Mr. Danford were willing to pay. Negotiations with Smith were pending when Mr. Danford was prostrated by his present sickness. We know too little of his affairs to make any statements or even guess as to the future. *Osage Free Press.*"

The Caldwell editor made no excuses for Danford, "We have no objection to the *Free Press* sympathizing with Mr. Danford in his present condition, but it won't do to make the 'brutal mob at Caldwell' responsible for all the ills Mr. Danford is now suffering.

Perhaps if the *Press* would put on its thinking cap, it might come to
the conclusion that Danford's habits had more to do with his
downfall and his sufferings than any action on the part of others. It
is the old story, old as Adam and Noah: It was the woman and wine
that did it."[191]

In March 1883 the Caldwell paper reported the continuing
Danford controversy. The editor said the people had been more
than patient in waiting to receive at least some of the money
Danford owed. Yet even at that late date, they saw no end in sight.
Other papers continued to take Danford's side, blaming Caldwell
creditors for treating Danford roughly.

Danford's attorney tried to get creditors to drop their claims.
The attorney's offer "amounted to the creditors giving up everything
and letting Mr. Danford go free with the booty in his pocket, and
opportunity to play the same game upon another unsuspecting
community.

"The medicine failed to work," the paper said, "and the man
who, while county attorney, had taken a fee from another whom he
should have prosecuted as a criminal, with his slick partner, quietly
took the morning train and returned to Wellington. The creditors,
on the other hand, proceeded to business at once, and decided to
enter criminal prosecution against Danford and his assistants in
rascality. Complaints have been prepared, and, we presume,
warrants issued before this, and if there is any justice, the creditors
will yet obtain a portion of their money and Danford will enjoy the
privileges of a felon's cell."[192]

By the end of March the two sides came to an agreement.
Danford turned all his Sumner County property over to the creditors
and dropped the $100,000 lawsuit against S.S. Richmond. The
property was valued at $76,000. The creditors in turn dropped all
their lawsuits against Danford.

"Of course, this will not give the creditors a very large
percentage on the amounts due them," said the Caldwell paper, "but
it is better than nothing, as they can now fully understand what they
are to rely upon."[193]

Though both sides settled, Caldwell seethed with bitter anger toward Danford for years to come. When William Cutler collected information for a Sumner County history published that year, citizens stonewalled him.

"The first banking house in Caldwell was the Merchants' and Drovers' Bank, which failed in November 1881," said Cutler. "No reliable particulars can be obtained concerning this institution, those who are supposed to know about it refusing information."[194]

Papers continued to report the whereabouts and dealings of J.S. Danford after this. The October 1, 1884 issue of *Arkansas City Traveler*, for example, found Danford up to his old tricks.

"Everybody in the country remembers Danford, the Caldwell banker, who stole a pile of money from his depositors a few years since," it said. "He has again come before the public, this time at Cheney, Washington Territory, where he stole $20,000, and skipped out to Victoria, B. C., from which place he openly defies his victims. He ought to be hung."

Though a wild gun battle and killing took place in Caldwell days after the bank closed, this bank failure received more press coverage than any other event for years to come. Trust of others hit an all-time low.

Caldwell citizens felt the impact of this bank failure more than they would have had a real bank robbery with armed bandits taken place. They had no way of recovering their money and it came from a trusted banker. They felt used. Had not lawmen restrained them, they would have left Danford hanging from a tree.

"This is the fourth murder..."

Though the 1881 cattle drive season ended in October, tension between Texas cowboys and Caldwell lawmen reached a violent peak in December 1881. Caldwell had just gone through its best cattle season ever. Town businessmen, especially saloon and dance hall owners, reveled in their new source of wealth. Town leaders enjoyed a healthy city income from fines these illegal businesses (prostitution and alcohol) paid.

Some cowboys remained in Caldwell after the drives. They may have been hoping for other kinds of work. Some may have considered becoming one of David L. Payne's "Oklahoma boomers," hoping to homestead in Indian Territory south of Caldwell.

But the longer cowboys stayed in Caldwell after the cattle season, the greater chance they had of doing battle with the law. During season the town kept a lid on the tension between cowboys and lawmen. Caldwell maintained a number of deputies to help the marshal. The mere presence of this organized group of lawmen helped maintain order. But when the season ended, Caldwell laid off most if not all the deputies.

Besides that, Texas cowboys tended to hate Kansas lawmen. Some of the hatred came from the Civil War. The cowboys treasured their independence, especially when it came to carrying a weapon. They hated to hand them over, as the Caldwell city ordinance demanded, especially when a Yankee with a badge demanded it. In the face of a weakened police force in off-season, the cowboys saw even less reason to oblige the Yankee lawman.

After Texas cowboy Jim Talbot and partners helped cattleman Captain Millet drive a herd to Caldwell that season, these cowboys decided to stay. Talbot even had his family with him. He rented a house from Daniel William Jones, who worked as a lawman during the cattle season.[195]

The longer the cowboys stayed in Caldwell the more restless they became. By December they had become a town nuisance. They kept their pistols strapped on. Sometimes in the late night when drinking and celebrating reached a peak, they would unloose a barrage of shots.

Friday night, December 16, 1881, real trouble brewed. Talbot and friends went to the opera house to watch the play, *Uncle Tom's Cabin*. Friends included Bob Bigtree, Dick Eddleman, Doug Hill, Tom Love, Jim Martin, and Bob Munson. They became loud and obnoxious, according to *Post* editor Tell W. Walton.

Editor Walton asked Talbot to quiet down his men. Talbot cursed. He threatened to fix Walton next day.

The cowboys continued drinking and celebrating after the play and into the next morning. At daybreak George Spear, who identified with the cowboys, shot off his revolver in the street. Other cowboys followed his lead.

Mike Meagher, who ran the Arcade Saloon nearby, heard the commotion and decided to do something about it, though he was no longer mayor. He headed to Marshal John Wilson's house and told him the situation. The two walked to the scene of the gunshots.

When they reached the center of town, they heard another gunshot. Tom Love had fired his gun in Moore Brothers Saloon. Wilson arrested Love and they headed toward jail. But the Talbot cowboys interfered. They threatened Wilson. Meagher tried to rescue him but ended up running up the opera stairs when the cowboys came after him. Witness W.H. Reily heard Talbot comment, "Meagher is the man we want, and Meagher is the man we will have." Tom Love also called out threats to Meagher before escaping.

The Talbot men regrouped at "Comanche Bill" Mankin's house near Fifth and Main. Nothing happened for several hours. Wilson worried that something might, so he sent a telegram to Mayor Cass Burrus in Wellington.

Around one that afternoon Wilson arrested Jim Martin for carrying a concealed weapon and resisting an officer. Martin appeared before a judge, who fined him. Martin didn't have the money, so Policeman Will D. Fossett escorted him to York and Company for the money.

On the way cowboys Jim Talbot, Tom Love, Bob Munson, and Dick Eddleman tried to rescue Martin. Fossett drew his gun and held them off. Talbot fired his gun as the cowboys retreated and called out, "Hide out, little ones."[196]

This started a battle between the cowboys and townsmen. Bullets riddled buildings as both sides opened up at Fifth and Main. The cowboys were to the north and west while Wilson, Meagher, and citizens were south and east of the intersection. Both parties worked their way east as they shot. Meagher and Wilson moved east between buildings south of Fifth till they entered the alley behind the buildings on the east side of Main.

Wilson warned Meagher to watch out for Talbot. The warning did no good. Talbot aimed his Winchester south toward Meagher and fired. Meagher gasped. "I'm hit and I'm hit hard," he told Wilson. Meagher still held a six-shooter in his right hand and a rifle under his left arm. Wilson helped him sit down on a box.

Ed F. Rathbun stood nearby and saw what happened. He went up to Meagher and asked, "Good God, Mike, are you hit?

"Yes," said Meagher. "Tell my wife I've got it at last."

The ball entered Meagher's right arm and passed through his lungs. Men carried Meagher to the barber shop, where he died within a half hour.[197]

When Talbot saw Meagher hit, he called to the other cowboys to mount up and leave. So the cowboys headed north to George Kalbfleisch's stables on Fourth. There they ordered Kalbfleisch at gunpoint to saddle up their horses. Meantime armed townsmen closed in from the south.

Red Light proprietor George Spear was saddling Talbot's horse near the saloon when a citizen's bullet stopped Spear, killing him instantly. Five of the cowboys mounted horses at Kalbfleisch's and rode east. Dick Eddleman and Tom Love were left behind with no horses to ride.

Someone shot one of the horses as the outlaws rode off. It forced Talbot to ride double on Doug Hill's horse. They along with Bob Munson, Jim Martin, and Bob Bigtree fled for their lives. Citizens gave chase.

Wilson's earlier telegram to Mayor Burrus in Wellington also got Sheriff Joe Thralls' attention. He and a 20-man posse arrived in Caldwell around three p.m., more than an hour after Talbot and the cowboys rode off.

Sheriff Thralls arrested Bob Love and Comanche Bill Mankin that night. Next morning, Sunday, December 18, Thralls arrested Dick Eddleman and Tom Delaney. The coroner's inquest exonerated Mankin and Delaney.

Stories spread on why the cowboys targeted Meagher. Some said Talbot sought revenge for Meagher killing Sylvester Powell in Wichita back in January 1877. Others believed Talbot sought revenge for George Flatt's death which many attributed to Meagher. Some thought Talbot's vendetta came from Meagher arresting him in March 1881. Another thought Talbot sought revenge for Meagher kicking him out of his saloon the day before the shooting.[198]

Animosity between Jim Talbot and Mike Meagher may have come down to the same problem in other cow towns. Meagher served as the epitome of the Yankee even though he was born in Ireland. He'd never worked as a cowboy. He spoke with an Irish brogue.

His former position as a lawman put him at odds with any cowboy. As a lawman he disarmed cowboys rather than identified with them. He fought for the Union in the Civil War. He owned saloons, not cattle.

Texas cowboys were southern rebels who fought as Confederates in the war. They treasured their freedom, their independence. That included freedom to carry a gun and use it when they felt like it.

Whether any of the stories about Talbot were true or not, he and Meagher had little in common. Meagher provided the perfect stereotypical object for Talbot's rage.

The five cowboys rode east out of Caldwell, crossed the railroad tracks and headed southeast. They met a man hauling hay to Caldwell and took a horse from him for the fifth rider. But another horse was injured. About a mile and a half southeast, the cowboys stopped at Bovine Park, headquarters of Wilbur Emery "Shorthorn" Campbell's ranch. There they took another horse.

"They rode into the yard and at the point of a Winchester commandeered a saddle horse from a group of men who were digging a well near the Campbell house. Mr. Campbell saw the incident from a window of his home, but was persuaded by Mrs. Campbell not to become involved. When the outlaws left, Mr. Campbell, well armed, started for Caldwell to mail some letters and papers. On the way he met a posse starting on the trail of the outlaws. He joined the posse and apparently by common consent became its leader."[199]

The cowboy outlaws had trouble staying ahead of the posse because their horses were nearly played out. They made it to the Deutcher Brothers horse ranch (later owned by Charles H. Moore) on Deer Creek about 10 miles southeast of Caldwell but not much further before their horses gave out.

The outlaws jumped off their horses and ran to a nearby canyon, guns blazing toward the posse close behind. The outlaws made it to a stone dugout where they took their stand.

The posse surrounded the gulch, but by then the sun was setting. This gave an advantage to the outlaws. Whenever the posse got in position to shoot they offered a clear target to the outlaws. They cast a clear outline in the setting sun.

W.E. Campbell determined to risk his life to catch the outlaws. He started sliding down one side of the gulch to get a closer shot. One of the cowboys happened to see him and showered him with shots. Some hit the mark. Campbell gasped, bleeding profusely. Somehow he retreated and others hauled him back to Caldwell. Only six people remained at the canyon to watch the outlaws since more than half the men left with Campbell.

Sometime after that Sheriff Joe Thralls and some of his deputies arrived. A number of other Caldwell citizens also later arrived. They guarded the gulch, hoping to catch the cowboys at daylight. When morning came they discovered the culprits had escaped in the night, probably not long after Campbell was shot.

Most citizens soon returned to Caldwell. Sheriff Joe Thralls, Deputy Frank Evans, R.W. Harrington, John W. Dobson, Sam Swayer, George Freeman, Abraham Rhoades, Tell Walton, and one other man remained. They searched the area for clues and went to surrounding cow camps to spread the word about the wanted outlaws. They then returned to Caldwell. Another party headed by George Brown also searched for the outlaws without success.[200]

Several leaders combined to offer a $1,100 reward for the outlaws, dead or alive. This included Mayor Cass Burrus, $500; Sheriff Joe Thralls, $200; W.E. Campbell, $200; and J.M. Steele (Meagher's brother-in-law), $200. Sheriff Thralls even put out descriptions of the cowboys.[201] Steele brought Meagher's body to Wichita where his grieving wife, Jenny, and a large crowd of friends attended the burial on Tuesday, December 20.[202]

A month later the *Caldwell Commercial* published a January 12, 1882 letter from the cowboy outlaws to the *Kansas City Times*. They denied being drunk or breaking any law before the shootout.

"The very reason the row came up," they said, "was that the honorable Marshal of Caldwell, John Wilson, was on a protracted drunk and stationed a posse of men in the Exchange saloon and told them to shoot every man that moved – that is, cowboys – then arming himself with two pistols, and then throwing them down on every one of the cowboys, telling them to throw up our hands, which we refused to do."[203]

None of the outlaws served time for the shootout and killing except Doug Hill (he served six months in the Wellington jail in 1887 for manslaughter). Jim Talbot was killed in Ukiah, California in 1896 by "parties unknown."[204]

Outsiders viewed Caldwell differently after the Talbot affair. Newspaper editors labeled it a lawless, deadly center where cowboys ruled. It became known as a place where "Hell is in session."

Citizens cringed at the image. For a while they tried to enforce prohibition and closed down some saloons. They especially raged against the Red Light. But expected business from the coming cattle drive season made Caldwell merchants hesitant about any major restrictions.

◊

With 1881 business booming, Caldwell leaders knew the town needed something to replace the defunct Merchants and Drovers Bank. Cattlemen saw the need. They financed the Stock Exchange Bank and a new $5,000 building on the south end of the business district to house it. The bank opened on December 24.

Not to be outdone, north side businessmen along with other cattlemen decided to open another financial house. In April 1882 they started the Caldwell Savings Bank. The town saw the sky as the only limits to its success. Optimism ran rampant.

Several prominent cattlemen came to Caldwell to oversee shipment of Texas cattle arriving from the 1882 drives. Among them were James D. Reed, J.W. Simpson, and Lee M. Kokernut. Other cattlemen heading herds up the Chisholm Trail included Jesse L. Hittson and Shanghai Pierce. This season Caldwell shipped 64,007 head, second only to Dodge City with 69,271. This proved to be Caldwell's peak cattle shipping year.[205]

As Caldwell entered its 1882 season, a neighboring county believed Caldwell would be the main center for the cattle trade. "The Atchison, Topeka and Santa Fe road has 308 locomotives and is constantly buying new ones," said the Arkansas City paper in Cowley County. "Caldwell will undoubtedly be the best market for Texas cattle in the state this year as it is the terminus of the great Chisholm trail over which three-fourths of the Texas cattle are driven, and easily accessible to the great distributing points, Kansas City, Chicago, and St. Louis, by rail and by telegraph."[206]

At the same time changes were taking place that would affect future business. Increasing numbers of cattlemen and farmers chose to fence their land with barbed wire. This left a rapidly shrinking area of open land to trail cattle. Also railroads in Texas began to lower their rates to attract Texas cattlemen who trailed herds north.

With record cattle shipments out of Caldwell in 1882, the town knew the large number of restless cowboys needed watching. The problem was, no lawman wanted the job. By March, George Brown got stuck with the job of town marshal.

The city council officially appointed 28-year-old George Brown, a bachelor who lived with his sister, Fannie, to replace John Wilson as marshal on April 10, 1882. A number of people questioned Brown's ability to fill that position in a town still suffering an image problem.

The town may not have had much choice. Marshals, as mentioned, were hard to find. Brown turned down the same position earlier before city leaders settled on John Wilson. Brown must have felt some civic duty to agree to the job this time. But he came into that position at a bad time.

Texas cowboys since the Meagher killing believed they had the upper hand in this wide open cattle shipping center. And Brown had little background in law enforcement. He had operated the Oyster Bay café and later worked as a gunsmith. But he never seemed cut out for being the town marshal.[207]

As summer approached, Caldwell filled up with cowboys and cattlemen. Citizens sensed the cattle business took precedence over everything else. Saloons prospered. Rowdy cowboys spent money freely. Merchants reveled in the business. Most townspeople recognized that cowboys ruled the place at least during the warm season. Even if George Brown were an outstanding lawman, he had his hands full. Cattle season had arrived in all its glory (and gore).

Townspeople felt increasing pressure to prove they could compete successfully with Dodge City. The *Post* editor jumped on the first chance he saw to boost Caldwell.

"The first herd of the season of 1882 arrived at this point Saturday [April 15], from Gonzales County, Texas," he said. "It is a herd of saddle and stock horses numbering 160, J. S. Tate, owner and driver. Mr. Tate says his stock came through in good shape; grass good all the way up; had no runs. He will hold at the stockyards till he closes out. Dodge City will please make a note of this: Caldwell gets the first herd! This herd was started for Dodge City, but Mr. Tate learned that Caldwell was the best market, and so drove here."[208]

◊

Around eight in the morning, Thursday, June 22, 1882, two Texas cowboys rode into town from Deer Creek, left their horses at a livery stable, and headed in to the Red Light Saloon. They had trailed with James F. Ellison's herd from the Red River up the Chisholm Trail. The two men, Edward Bean (alias J.D. "Jess" Green) and his brother, James Bean (alias Steven Green) drew attention from Caldwell citizens as they entered the Red Light.

One observer noticed they were armed, or at least one of them carried a pistol. The citizen reported it to Marshal Brown, who was on Main Street gathering signatures for some petitions about voting bonds. Brown had no desire to enter the Red Light alone, so he asked Constable Willis Metcalf to back him up.

Inside the Red Light the two lawmen walked upstairs and ran into the Bean brothers and one other cowboy. Edward "Jess" Bean

129

held a pistol. Marshal Brown quickly grabbed Beans arm that held the gun and told him to give it up.

"Let go of me," Bean yelled. Brown pinned Bean's arm against the wall.

Another cowboy grabbed Metcalf by the throat, pushed him back into a corner, and told him to hold up his hands while the third cowboy held a gun on him. A fourth man suddenly jumped out of a room across the stairway and yelled at Brown.

"Turn him loose!"

Brown turned toward the man. Bean saw his chance. He twisted his gun hand around, pointing the pistol at Brown's head, and fired. Marshal Brown slumped to the floor, dead before landing.

The third man held his gun on others as the two brothers escaped. The Beans rode south and east out of Caldwell. Local businessmen resisted the posse's efforts to find out more about the cowboy outlaws. And Mayor Albert M. Colson ran into a roadblock when he tried to gain control of saddle horses at a hitching post to quickly chase the Beans. The owners refused to give them up.

The Bean brothers rode till they came to Andrew Drumm's ranch, where they ate and got fresh mounts. Then they returned to the T5 ranch (Texas Land and Cattle Company) where they stayed for eight days before heading back to Texas.[209]

The posse found out the cowboys were from Ellison's herd and the herd boss was a man named McGee. Some said the Bean brothers were French Canadians from Collingswood, Ontario. And they had a history of lawlessness. Texas Rangers called them "the gamest desperadoes in Texas."[210]

The Bean brothers hid out in Texas. The June 29, 1882 *Caldwell Commercial* included their descriptions in hopes of capturing them. But Sheriff Joe Thralls felt he had to do more. He wrote a letter to Kansas Governor John P. St. John.

After telling about Marshal George Brown's murder, Thralls said, "Now are you not authorized to offer a reward of $500 apiece for their arrest and delivery to the Sheriff of Sumner Co? We are having so much of this kind of work it does seem as though the

State should offer a good reward for some of these 'Texas killers' and outlaws. This is the fourth murder within the last year at Caldwell and Hunnewell and no reward offered by State for any of them."

Governor St. John answered on July 6, 1882 with a Governor' Proclamation. In it he offered a $1,000 reward, $500 for each of the Bean brothers, for their arrest and conviction.[211]

The last two cattle drive seasons confirmed Caldwell's image among neighboring communities. They believed Caldwell no longer had control over lawless cowboys. They believed the town had become wide open, allowing unlimited alcohol, celebrations, and gunplay. Both the Meagher and the Brown killings proved it to them.

In Wellington, the June 29 *Sumner County Press* blamed Caldwell's troubles on whiskey and prostitutes. The July 6 *Caldwell Post* responded, pointing out exaggerations. It didn't stop the critics.

Sheriff Thralls added $400 to the governor's reward. Still the Bean brothers roamed free. And criticism continued. Sometimes the Caldwell paper met it with sarcasm, pointing out hypocrisy among the critics. But everyone knew the best way to end criticism would be to catch the killers. Thralls did what he could and so did Texas lawmen.

"It took a man with a great deal of nerve."

"Prohibition prohibits in Winfield, we know, because the *Courier* says it does," said the September 14, 1882 *Caldwell Commercial*. "In further confirmation of this fact, it is our special privilege to relate the adventures of a Caldwell man while on a visit to his former town last week.

"Upon the arrival of the Caldwellite in Winfield, he accidentally ran across an old acquaintance, who at once proceeded to introduce him to the old residents. The first one they ran across was a popular merchant on Main Street, who upon being informed that the subject of our sketch was from Caldwell, grunted out, 'What? From Caldwell? Then you want something substantial,' and at once preceded to a shoebox from which he extracted a demijohn, the contents of which smelled and tasted like whiskey.

"Pursuing the rounds, the next place he dropped into was a dry goods store kept by a former acquaintance who wanted to know where our friend was living, and upon being informed that Caldwell was his present place of abode, exclaimed, 'H--l, you must be dry," and at once produced a bottle . . .

"And so it went on, one place offering 'strait racket,' another 'budweiser,' another 'export,' another 'St. John amendment,' etc. until the Caldwellian was fain to say that he had met one Frank Jones on the train. From him he had learned to adorn the truth. He couldn't help but say he was from Caldwell. But the truth was, no such place had an existence upon the map.

"After such a confession as that, the jig was up. And from that time on until he was about ready to leave town, no one offered him a dram or hinted that there was such a thing as whiskey in the world unless it might be in the cellar of a deacon or an elder."

◊

All the bad publicity made Caldwell citizens more determined than ever to shed this rambunctious cow town image. When Charlie Davis killed Red Light Saloon owner George Wood[s] back in August 1881, the place almost closed down. The 1882 booming cattle business kept it open another year. But the George Brown killing in June finally sounded the death knoll. The Red Light finally closed its doors to alcohol, never to reopen.

◊

Nearly four months passed before lawmen caught up with George Brown's killers. The October 19 *Caldwell Post* reported that lawmen caught the Bean brothers in Wise County, Texas. Caldwell lawman Frank Evans, who brought the outlaws back to Kansas, gave details in the October 26 issue.

The Bean brothers had recently moved to Wise County after shooting a deputy marshal in Smith County, where they had lived after killing Brown. The deputy marshal killing brought a $250 reward for the capture of the Bean brothers. When some cowboys killed a Wise County, Texas farmer's cow on Tuesday, October 10, a constable and posse followed their trail. The lawmen soon caught up with the cowboys, who turned out to be the Bean brothers.

The posse "discovered the horses of the outlaws in a pasture, staked out, the fence still being down," Evans said in the October 26 *Post*. "The constable arranged the men on either side of the gap . . . After waiting something over an hour, Jim [Bean] was seen approaching the gap, walking leisurely, with a six-shooter belt hanging over his shoulder.

"The constable allowed him to approach within ten steps of him when he raised up with his shot gun, covered his man and commanded him to throw up his hands and surrender. Jim raised his hand, level with his shoulders, and quick as thought pulled his six-shooter and fired on the constable, the ball grazing his temples and knocking him out of time.

"[Bean] then turned and started to run, but the constable soon came to and was up and after him, but forgot his shotgun. The constable's posse rose and began firing at Jim, and after a chase of a hundred yards succeeded in putting a ball into his back. The constable had emptied his six-shooter after Jim, and just as Jim fell his brother Ed came in sight carrying two shotguns and a Winchester. The constable skipped back to his friends. The [Bean] boys got away and the posse would not follow the constable."

The Bean boys headed back to their family's place about 10 miles away. Lawmen hired a boy to follow them. The boy stayed on their trail for two days and nights before pinpointing their location. By then it was the middle of the night. Jim Bean's back wound left him cold, forcing the outlaws to build a fire.

The boy snuck away and quickly reported his discovery to the constable. The constable and his men, armed with shotguns and Winchesters, surrounded the camp. When they were about 30 yards away, the constable stood up and aimed his shotgun at the sleeping outlaws.

He called out for them to surrender. No one answered. He called out again and noticed movement but no answer. He called out a third time. The Bean brothers leaped up and blasted their shotguns toward the lawmen. The outlaws missed their target.

"The constable at once said, 'Turn her loose, boys,' and a perfect storm of bullets rained upon the outlaws," said Evans. "Ed fell down instantly with two bullet holes through his head obliquely, one from his right cheek coming out back of his left ear and the other from his left cheek through behind his right ear.

"Jim fell and remained unconscious for several hours. His wounds consisted of fourteen bullet holes in his body made by thirteen balls, one passing through his leg. A Winchester ball struck him in the back to the right of the spinal column and lodged near the skin under his right arm. Another Winchester ball cut the extreme point of his chin, thence to his collarbone, and lodged under his left shoulder blade. One ball struck just to the left of the center of the forehead, entering the skin and flattening against the skull bone. This ball is supposed to have knocked him out of time. He had several bullet holes in his breast, scattered around promiscuously and in various other parts of his body."[212]

On Wednesday morning, October 18, Frank Evans left Decatur, Texas (a few miles northwest of Dallas) with Jim Bean and arrived in Wellington on Saturday, October 21. Bean lay in the county jail two weeks. On Sunday, November 5, he died from his wounds.

On Tuesday, November 7, Sheriff Thralls sent another letter to Governor St. John. He told him about the capture, arrest, and death of both outlaws.

"That ends the course of the two murderers of George Brown," Thralls said. "Now what is necessary for us to do to get the State reward, which goes to their captors in Texas? We can give you several affidavits of his own admission to killing Brown. The one that died in our Jail is the one who fired the fatal shot while the other, his [brother] was present and assisted by keeping off Brown's deputy and came near to shooting him. He told the boys in Jail (five of them) the circumstance of their flight after the murder . . .

"We are asking this for the Texas Officers who have done good work in the case – And what was dangerous work, in good faith, and at some expense. Now I would like to see them rewarded to make our part of the contract good."[213]

◊

On June 27, five days after George Brown's death, Caldwell Mayor Albert M. Colson and the city council appointed B.P. "Bat" Carr the new marshal and Bedford B. Wood his assistant.[214] The town desperately needed a good marshal to gain control over the increasing number of reckless and sometimes lawless cowboys.

Within a week, on Monday, July 3, Henry Newton Brown replaced B.B. Wood as Carr's assistant.[215]

The town held strong views about the need to have a professional police force. They hoped never to make the mistake of hiring someone not prepared for brute force in a gun battle. Some felt leaders made that mistake when they hired George Brown.

How leaders decided on Henry Newton Brown has never come to light. He may have sold himself, though this flew in the face of his taciturn personality. A more likely possibility points to people who knew him.

Leading businessman Charles F. Colcord believed his father, Col. W.L. Colcord, and cattleman Andrew Drumm played a key role. "Caldwell at that time was one of the worst towns in the country, and it took a man with a great deal of nerve to be its marshal," Colcord explained. "My father and Major Drumm, knowing Henry Brown's great nerve and fearlessness, recommended him to the Caldwell folks. They sent for him while he was at my camp and gave him a job as deputy under Bat Carr, who was later discharged. Henry Brown was then made marshal."[216]

Carr marked a new era in Caldwell, being both an outsider and a professional lawman. So was his new assistant, Henry Newton Brown.

George Freeman described Carr as five feet eight, 180 pounds. "He was usually seen dressed in a uniform of dark navy blue with polished gilt trimming and brass buttons," Freeman said. "On his finger he wore a handsome ring set with precious stones; in his hand he carried a polished cane and upon his breast a large silver star with the words, 'Bat Carr, Marshal,' inscribed on it."[217]

Carr left a mixed impression on others. He seemed sophisticated and mannerly, but also dangerous. "His height of ambition was to be feared by men," Freeman said. He added that Carr "was looked upon as a necessary evil to straighten the lower class of humanity which paraded the streets of Caldwell."[218]

Caldwell citizens still hoped for the best. They raised $75 from businessmen and bought "a brace of six-shooters." Businessman Col. Jennison, representing town businesses, gave them to Carr on July 12. "I present you with these weapons," Jennison said, "not that we would encourage the use of them, but that you may better protect the rights of property and life, and maintain the dignity and honor of the city and your office as marshal."[219]

The same issue of the *Post* told about Carr facing an armed man. The man tried to draw on him but Carr beat him to the draw with his .45 and disarmed him.

Carr didn't disappoint the town. He seemed to know what merchants wanted in a law officer. When a gambler tried to beat a cowboy out of his last dollar, Carr came to the cowboy's defense. "Our present force seem to comprehend the fact that men coming into the town are not to be openly robbed without any interference on their part," said the *Commercial*, "and we are glad of it."[220]

Carr sometimes used fists instead of guns. He and Henry Brown broke up two fights in late August without drawing their weapons. The paper commended the lawmen. "...We must congratulate them upon being pioneers in the new order of things that makes the six-shooter in this community of no more account than a toy pistol."[221]

But Bat Carr used force when he needed to. On Monday, September 4, a drunk cowboy named William St. John caused a ruckus in town. He was roping Dr. William A. Noble's sheep near the doctor's house when Carr came by. Carr quickly disarmed St. John and jailed him. "William took his departure, poorer in purse, but doubtless happy in the consciousness that he had a 'good time'."[222]

Carr continued to oppose gamblers who tried to cheat cowboys out of the payroll. He arrested some for carrying concealed weapons. He arrested others for running games with unfair advantage.[223]

Citizens' admiration of Marshal Carr grew by leaps and bounds. The first week of October they gave him a gold badge.

"It took a man with a great deal of nerve."

"It is solid gold in the form of a shield suspended from a plate at the top by chains," said the *Post*. "The lettering is in black enamel and bears the inscription, 'Batt Carr, City Marshal, Caldwell, Kan.' On the reverse is, 'Presented by the Citizens of Caldwell.' . . . Batt is deserving of the best regards of the citizens of Caldwell by reason of his excellent management of the rougher element that is common in any new community, and they take this method of showing it. The cost of the jewel was over $75, and was bo't through Henry Auling, our jeweler, by a few of our businessmen and stockmen."[224]

Carr then took a leave of absence starting Monday, October 16. He headed back to his hometown of Colorado City, Texas. In the meantime Henry Brown replaced Carr as town marshal and appointed Ben Wheeler as his assistant.

In Colorado, Carr put six houses up for sale and closed his ties there. He returned Thursday, November 2 ready to settle down in Caldwell. But before getting back to business, he gave Mayor Colson a gold-headed cane that he had brought with him.

Bat Carr definitely saw a bright future for himself in Caldwell. His popularity had peaked out. But he still had to deal with mundane affairs of the town.

A well-known cow town tramp, Robert Gilmore (better known as Bobby Gill), happened to land in Caldwell that fall. For a few days, Gilmore stayed sober. During that time he dressed up and went to a church service. And he behaved admirably. This turned some heads, more so than if he'd gotten into a drunken brawl.

It seemed to bother professional gamblers more than it bothered peace-loving citizens. The gamblers may have felt threatened by his peaceful behavior or they may have been anticipating future trouble. Or perhaps the Caldwell paper reported only part of what happened and added its usually tongue-in-cheek style.

"The next morning the gamblers insisted on Bobby leaving town," the paper reported. "He had disgraced the profession by going to church, and they couldn't stand it. So they raised some money to pay for his fare to the home of all such refugees, Dodge City, and at three o'clock, Bat Carr escorted him to the depot in style and saw him safely ensconced in a reclining chair, and we hope, that by this time, he is under the protecting care of Mayor Webster."[225]

Carr continued to arrest gamblers, hoping to limit their power over what he considered victims of their dishonesty.[226] That more than any other type of arrest marked his reign as marshal. This stood well with farmers and local citizens. And it gave him confidence in his position.

Carr took another leave of absence in early December. He went to Dallas, Texas where he wedded. Then an odd thing happened. On December 21, while Carr was still in Texas, Caldwell leaders appointed Henry Brown as the new town marshal. Rumors later spread about why.

Caldwell citizen Joe Wiedeman more that four decades after the event said Henry Brown forced Carr to resign.[227] Historian Richard L. Lane believed the Caldwell city council fired Carr as a result of complaints from local politician I.N. Cooper.[228] Whatever the reason, Carr's reign as marshal came to an abrupt end. It now came down to Henry Newton Brown and Ben Wheeler to keep a tight reign on a wild town.

Bat Carr could be proud of what he accomplished. In his entire time as marshal in Caldwell's busiest cattle season, he never had to kill anyone. That coming after several years of regular killings in Caldwell said a lot about Carr's abilities as a lawman.

"The boys would make excellent constables."

Henry Newton Brown started his career as Caldwell marshal with plenty of experience, most of it unknown to residents. Born in 1857, somewhere between 1873 and 1875 he left his uncles farm near Rolla, Missouri to seek adventure in the west. He worked as a cowboy and a buffalo hunter before joining up with Billy the Kid's gang in New Mexico. During his cowboy days he killed his first man, according to Texas cowboy and later detective Charles Siringo.[229] While with Billy the Kid, Brown took part in several killings and was indicted on three.

When they became wanted men, Billy the Kid's gang, including Brown, left New Mexico with stolen horses and headed to Tascosa, Texas. A little later they went 20 miles south to the LX ranch. There Charles Siringo met Henry Brown and the others and remained friendly for a time.[230]

Before the end of 1878 Billy the Kid and Tom O'Folliard headed back to New Mexico while Henry Brown, Fred Waite, and John Middleton remained in Texas. Middleton soon headed to Kansas while Brown went with Waite to northeastern Indian Territory before heading back to Tascosa in spring, 1879. But Brown didn't stay long before continuing on to New Mexico. Charles Siringo said Brown worked a few months as "boss of a cow camp" but had to leave after being involved in a shooting.[231]

Brown went back to Tascosa where he stayed till 1881. During that time he worked for a while as a cowboy at the LIT ranch near town. Late in 1879 he switched jobs, hiring on at the Campbell-

Ledger ranch north of town. This job included chasing horse thieves. In 1880 he became a lawman in Tascosa.

That year (1880) Tascosa became the county seat of Oldham County. The county sheriff, Cape Willingham, and one his officers, Joe Mason, had connections with Dodge City, Kansas. Willingham had worked as an LS ranch cowboy and later ran the Dodge City mail route. Joe Mason had served as a lawman in Dodge in 1877 and 1878. Henry Brown likely heard stories from both of them about Dodge City and other Kansas cow towns.

Brown worked for Sheriff Willingham till the middle of 1881, when the sheriff fired him because he "was always wanting to fight and get his mane up."[232] Brown hired on at the LIT ranch but was again fired for the same reason. After that Brown worked as a cowboy in Indian Territory, becoming a familiar figure among cowboys and cattlemen.

At this time the northern portion of Indian Territory, known as the Cherokee Outlet, was filling up with cattlemen who paid grazing fees to the Cherokee Nation, which owned the land. These cattlemen from the Cherokee Outlet met in Caldwell in the spring of 1880 and formed an unofficial group to better protect their interests. Three years later, on March 6, 7, and 8, 1883 in Caldwell this group officially organized as the Cherokee Strip Live Stock Association.

When Henry Newton Brown began work as a cowboy for ranches in the Cherokee Outlet, his reputation spread among these cattlemen. And when Caldwell suffered its crisis of a murdered marshal (George Brown) in the middle of its busiest cattle season (1882), town leaders wanted to take no chances. They quickly spread the word of their need for an efficient lawman.

They wanted the best, toughest, most experienced lawmen they could find to keep a lid on rowdy cowboys during this golden age of the cattle trade. They found their man in Texas. The man, Bat Carr, had the reputation they were looking for.

They also found Henry Brown in the Cherokee Outlet with a reputation to match. They didn't need much help from Col. W.L. Colcord and Andrew Drumm to decide.[233]

Brown liked to live dangerously or at least was willing to for a possible reward. In September 1882 he temporarily resigned as Carr's deputy to join Sheriff Joe Thralls' posse. Thralls' was headed into Indian Territory after Jim Talbot and his gang. Talbot had shot and killed Mayor Mike Meagher back in December 1881. Brown returned after 17 days of unsuccessful pursuit.[234]

When Brown replaced Carr as Caldwell marshal at the end of 1882, town leaders placed the same confidence in him as they had in Carr. And Brown's first act as marshal bolstered their confidence. He chose another Texan, Ben Wheeler (real name Ben Robertson), with a similar reputation for his assistant. Proof of the city's confidence in them came in the way of pay. Town leaders doubled the marshal's salary. It went from $50 to $100 a month. The deputy's salary jumped to $75 a month.

Wheeler (Robertson) already had served temporarily as assistant marshal and Brown as marshal when Carr took a leave of absence in October 1882. Robertson used several aliases. In his first marriage he used Burton, and his second, Wheeler. He left both for a wilder life in Caldwell, where he used the name, Wheeler, from then on.

The different sized Brown and Wheeler (Brown was five-foot-six, Wheeler over six feet tall) had similar personalities. "Brown and Wheeler both had quiet and restrained personal habits, both had desperate backgrounds which they wanted to keep hidden, and both could handle a gun," said Bill O'Neal.[235]

Only days after Brown became marshal, town leaders surprised him. On Monday, January 1, 1883, they convinced him to enter the York-Parker-Draper Mercantile store. There the city presented him with a .44-40 octagonal barreled Winchester rifle with a pistol grip. Its polished black walnut stock had an engraved oval-shaped gold plate on it which read, "Presented to City Marshall/ H.N. Brown/ For valuable services rendered/ in behalf of the Citizens of CALDWELL KAS/ A.N. Colson Mayor Dec 1882".[236]

Brown, stunned and self-conscious, thanked the town. Citizens figured they had another wild season ahead and wanted the marshal in the best attitude possible. This did the trick. Brown played his role masterfully.

Brown and Wheeler dealt with small as well as large problems. On January 7, 1883 Ben Wheeler caught a man trying to hide stolen articles. Never mind he stole women's underwear and jewelry. The man ended up spending time in the Sumner County jail.[237]

On Wednesday, January 31, Henry Brown took a month's leave to visit relatives in Rolla, Missouri. While in Missouri, he spoke to the newspaper editor, telling him about his work as a lawman. He claimed to be the only marshal in Caldwell to have tamed the cowboys. Brown wore his six-guns in Rolla, perhaps hoping to impress his Missouri relatives and friends with the dangerous job he held in a wild Kansas cow town.[238]

This came shortly before the cowboy's heroic image. In fact the public image of cowboys then fell far short of that. Perhaps transient bums on horseback who endangered the public with six-gun antics better described them in the early 80s.

"The Wild Western hero as a cowboy, who in the twentieth century has become the dominant type, first appeared in the wake of Buffalo Bill in the late 1880s," said historian Henry Nash Smith. "As a press agent for the Wild West show [Prentiss] Ingraham strove to offset the bad reputation which cowboys had with the public."[239]

Henry Brown may have still felt many in Caldwell saw him as nothing more than a cowboy with a badge. Unlike Bat Carr, Brown had worked as a cowboy and he had little or no money saved to call his own.

Carr not only seemed more sophisticated, but also had more money. Carr moved to Wellington in 1883 and tried to buy land near Caldwell later that year.[240] Brown probably noticed this. In fact, this may have spurred Brown on to get married, buy a house, and acquire some fast money. This would set him apart from other cowboys.

Brown returned from his vacation in Missouri on Saturday, March 3. To bolster his positive image in Caldwell, Brown served as a guard at a picnic on Sunday, March 18.

◊

On Thursday, March 22, 1883, Deputy Marshal Wheeler faced flying bullets. This time it involved a leading citizen. Dr. William A. Noble got drunk in a saloon, got mad at a man named Charles Everhart, and started shooting. The first shot missed, the second hit Everhart in the left side of the chest and exited his back. Everhart turned and Noble's third shot hit him in the back and came out above the collarbone. By then Wheeler reached Noble and yanked the gun out of his hand.[241]

Everhart lived. Noble went on trial and was granted a continuance. Everhart later left Caldwell. Nothing more came of the trial.

◊

The year 1883 saw more competition between the town's "north enders" (mostly merchants) and "south enders" (mostly cattlemen). Soon each group had their own hotel, the Southwestern for the "north enders" and the Leland for the "south enders."[242]

After the elections on Tuesday, April 3, the city council reappointed Brown and Wheeler to their positions. A week later, on Tuesday, April 10, around 11 p.m., Brown and Wheeler rode to Hunnewell with Deputy U.S. Marshal Cash Hollister.

Hollister needed help in chasing down some horse thieves. At Hunnewell the three lawmen added Hunnewell Marshal Jackson and Sumner County Deputy Sheriff William "Elzy" Thralls to their group.

The five lawmen continued southeast of Hunnewell till they reached the horse thieves' camp, which they surrounded. Those in the horse thief group included a man named Ross, his wife,

145

daughter, two sons, a daughter-in-law, and her child. Several others happened to be traveling with the Ross family, though they weren't involved with stealing horses.

At dawn, the lawmen called out to the Ross family to surrender. The Ross's answered with gunfire from Winchesters. Both sides continued shooting for half an hour. During that time the oldest son was killed and the younger one wounded in several places. The family then surrendered. The lawmen hauled the dead boy to Hunnewell and the others to Wellington.[243]

By this time cattle business was picking up in Caldwell. The April 12 issue of the *Commercial* said "Peter Stewart bought the Jones & Prescott cattle the other day, paying $12,500. On Tuesday last [April 10] he shipped three car loads of beeves out of the herd and made a contract with Mr. Mitchell north of town and near the Chikaskia to feed the balance of the herd."

◊

On Monday morning, May 14, Marshal Brown used deadly force. A Pawnee Indian, Spotted Horse, came to Caldwell in a two-horse wagon with a squaw during that weekend and camped out at a vacant lot between Main and Market Street.

On Monday morning a little after six he went to the Long Branch Restaurant with his squaw and asked for breakfast. The proprietor refused. Spotted Horse then went to Moreland House where he got cold meat and bread. Next he went to E.H. Beals' house on Market north of Fifth.

He walked in on the family as they were beginning breakfast and demanded food. Beals' wife asked the Indians to leave. They did, but Spotted Horse then returned and put his hand on Mrs. Beals' head. Mr. Beals jumped up and told him to get out. Spotted Horse pulled out a revolver. Mr. Beals told him to go outside with him and they would settle it there.

Outside the Indian again pulled out his gun. Beals picked up a spade. Another man, Grant Harris, interceded. The Indians left and walked into the back door of the Long Branch. Meanwhile Beals told Marshal Brown of the trouble.

Spotted Horse next went in Morris' grocery store while his squaw went back to the wagon. Marshal Brown came on the scene while Spotted Horse was in the grocery.

Gordon W. "Pawnee Bill" Lillie, then 23 and working as a waiter in a Caldwell restaurant, heard about the trouble and headed to the area. He knew Spotted Horse and could speak the language. He believed he could quell the dispute. Lillie went in the Long Branch and asked what was going on.

While still in the Long Branch, Pawnee Bill heard four shots. He ran to the store where he heard the shots and found Spotted Horse on the floor and Marshal Brown holstering his gun. "Lillie always believed that had he reached the store ahead of the marshal, he could have saved the Indians' life," said Glenn Shirley.[244]

The story told by witnesses said Marshal Brown entered the grocery, saw Spotted Horse, and asked him to go with him to Mr. Covington, an interpreter. Spotted Horse either didn't understand him or didn't want to go. He reached for his revolver.

Brown drew his gun and shot it in the air as a warning. Spotted Horse ignored it. Brown shot three more times, the last shot hitting the Indian above the right eye and coming out the back of his head.

This action came just as the 1883 cattle season was coming into full swing. Businessmen crossed their fingers hoping nothing else would happen to scare off business.

Contrary to businessmen's worries, the Spotted Horse incident had a positive effect on rowdy cowboys. When the trail drivers heard how Marshal Brown dealt with the Indian, they had no desire to tangle with the feisty lawman.

◊

Around the time of the Spotted Horse killing, Caldwell received good news. The Cherokee Strip Live Stock Association, which had begun as an official group in March, made an agreement with the

Cherokee Council. The Cherokee Nation granted the cattlemen a five-year lease at an annual rate of $100,000 a year.

"The advantage of this lease to Caldwell will be immense," the paper said, "because it gives an assurance of a steady and profitable business. Having an assurance that they will not be disturbed for the next five years, many of the stock men will make their homes in our city, and with their wealth and influence contribute largely toward making it one of the most substantial towns in the West."[245]

On Tuesday, May 29, the CSLSA board appointed Mayor A.M. Colson as chairman of the Board of Arbitration. The association decided to survey the Cherokee Outlet land to establish the area of each of the cattlemen. They divided the outlet into three divisions, east, central, and west, and assigned different association members to oversee the survey in each division.

Milton H. Bennett and James W. Hamilton oversaw the eastern division "from the 96th meridian on the east to the Chisholm Trail on the west and from the state line on the north to the southern line of the Cherokee Territory." Major Andrew Drumm and Ben S. Miller oversaw the land "from the Chisholm Trail on the east to a line running north and south on the west line of the Texas Land and Cattle Company on the West." Charles H. Eldred and Edward Wylie Payne oversaw "from the line running north and south on the west line of the Texas Land and Cattle Company to the 100th meridian west and from the south line of Kansas on the north to the south line of the Cherokee country."[246]

The good news for the CSLSA offset a disappointing year for "through" cattle (Texas cattle coming up the Chisholm Trail) to Caldwell. While the 1882 season saw 64,000 cattle shipped, the 1883 figure dropped to 28,379 head. Cattlemen spread the blame. Drought, increased fencing, and a late winter blizzard, all played a part. Dodge City again dominated the "through" cattle business with 74,237 head being shipped that year.[247]

The same day the CSLSA decided to survey the outlet, Brown, Wheeler, and Hollister had a minor run-in with a small-time thief. A 25-year-old cowboy named John Caypless stole a saddle. The lawmen found out and made him haul it back from Fall Creek where it was hidden. Caypless spent time in the Wellington county jail.[248]

Overall, the Caldwell lawmen performed well during the 1883 season. Between March and July they generated $1,296 in fines, some $421 more than their salary.[249]

An example of their efficiency came on Tuesday, August 7. When three cowboys left Caldwell with blazing guns, Brown and Wheeler chased them down. The lawmen hauled the cowboys before Judge T.H.B. Ross, who fined them. This time the cowboys rode out of town quietly.[250]

Brown and Wheeler seemed to make up a perfect team in corralling lawbreakers and taming Caldwell. Merchants and town leaders couldn't be more pleased. Caldwell was building up a reputation as a place one could visit without getting shot at.

Brown had made a good choice in Wheeler. Brown must have known what he was doing because Wheeler provided the perfect complement. Townsmen from the Mayor to merchants liked Brown though many cowboys didn't. On the other hand, Wheeler identified with the cowboys.

Ben Wheeler even had cowboys help him play a joke on one Caldwell merchant. Cherokee Outlet cowboy Laban Records liked to tell about the incident. He remembered in the early 1880s when he was inside a Caldwell saloon just north of Louis Segerman's Restaurant.

Segerman, a short heavy-set German, liked to take naps on a bench in front of his business during breaks. This day the street was muddy from recent rain. The street also had holes in it next to the boardwalk, a result of horses pawing the ground while parked at hitching posts.

Wheeler saw his chance. As Segerman soundly napped on the bench, Wheeler gently rolled him over till he fell off and plopped into one of the mud holes. Quickly, Wheeler ran inside the nearby saloon, told a few cowboys what he did, and asked them to play along. He then exited the saloon along with the cowboys.

Segerman meanwhile was struggling out of the mud hole and sputtering revenge on the culprit who rolled him. He spotted Wheeler. They looked at each other and Wheeler yelled, "What's going on here? What does this mean?"

Segerman blurted out about someone pushing him in the mud. Wheeler drew his six-gun, pointed his finger at Laban Records, and said, "Did you do that?"

"No!" Records answered.

Wheeler then lectured all the cowboys around him, warning them never to do such a thing. Segerman, now pumped up, said, "Shoot 'em mit a bullet!"

"That's right, Louie, shoot 'em mit a bullet!" Wheeler repeated.[251]

While Wheeler could joke with cowboys, Henry Brown remained hostile to them. In fact some cowboys saw Brown as an enemy. Cowboy Laban Records, who worked for the Spade ranch (Bates and Company) northeast of the T5, had worked with Brown before Brown became Caldwell's marshal.

"Brown and I had worked together on the Spade ranch," Records said, "and his work didn't suit me. I told Sam Fling. He discharged Brown and that made him sore. Brown didn't know that I was the source of his downfall. He was so mean to his horses; he had no mercy. I never could stand to see a person abusing a dumb beast."[252]

But word spread and Brown eventually found out Records' roll. So Records feared retaliation. But luck was with him. The next time Records trailed a herd to Caldwell and met up with the lawman, Brown seemed to hold no grudge.

Cowboy Oliver Nelson, then with the T5 ranch, also remembered a run-in with Henry Brown. One day he traveled by buckboard to Caldwell, bringing a sick friend to Dr. Noble. Nelson then headed to a feed barn to stall his mules.

"At the barn door stood Henry Brown, the marshal," said Nelson. I said, 'How do you do, Henry.' He just stood and looked. I passed on and he followed about ten steps behind. Somehow it seemed suspicion would loom up whenever a T5 horse came to town. I learned later they had it in for us all, and he'd said he would make them T5 men lay off their guns or kill every damned one of them. But I didn't have a gun; seldom carried one."[253]

◊

Nearly everyone in the Caldwell area held Marshal Henry Newton Brown in high esteem when it came to keeping order. Townspeople trusted him with their lives and, in the case of the Cherokee Strip Live Stock Association, with their money.

In the Fall of 1883 the Association had a big problem. They needed to ship $50,000 in cold cash across Indian Territory, then part of the wildest country in the nation. This looked like a golden opportunity for any outlaw band worth their salt. And the CSLSA knew it. But it had to be done. The reason dated back to March.

Ever since the Texas cattle drives began, cattlemen increasingly used the Cherokee Outlet south of Caldwell to graze their stock before shipping them east. As mentioned earlier, in 1880 these cattleman met in Caldwell and loosely organized to combat growing problems with both settlers and Indians.

Between 1880 and 1883 the cattlemen began paying grazing fees to the Cherokee Nation, which owned the land. Settlers complained because they knew the cattlemen had no legal right to stay on the land. Settlers knew this because when they tried to homestead there, government troops kicked them out. Indians believed the cattlemen took advantage of them since the grazing fees were only a fraction of what the land was worth.

On March 6, 7, and 8 cattlemen took a major step in solving this problem. They met in Caldwell and officially incorporated under the laws of Kansas as the Cherokee Strip Live Stock Association. They chose Ben S. Miller as president, John A. Blair as secretary, and Milton H. Bennett as treasurer.

Their by-laws laid out rules for boundary lines among the different cattlemen, branding marks, and dues members must pay.

They proposed leasing the land from the Cherokee Nation to gain a stronger legal position.

The cattlemen negotiated with Cherokee Nation Chief Dennis W. Bushyhead, who met with the Cherokee Council in Tahlequa in May. The Council decided to offer the cattlemen a five-year lease at $100,000 a year, to be paid semi-annually in advance. The Cherokees demanded payment in silver. The Council signed the agreement in July and it went into effect on October 1, 1883.[254]

By Friday night, September 28, CSLSA Treasurer Milt Bennett collected more than enough lease money for the first payment to the Cherokee Nation. The logistical problem remained. How could Bennett safely deliver $50,000 in silver to the Cherokee Nation's headquarters in Tahlequah?

The cattlemen sought Caldwell Marshal Henry Newton Brown's help. They looked to him for maximum protection in a most dangerous situation. He would have to guard $50,000 worth of silver (about one-and-a-half tons) through Indian Territory.[255]

This territory was perhaps the most dangerous area in the country at that time. "Between the end of the Civil War and the turn of the century, more deputy marshals were killed in the line of duty than at any other time in their history," said author Robert Sabbag. "Between 1872 and 1896, 103 deputy marshals were killed in what at that time was known as Indian Territory."[256]

Cattlemen looked to Henry Brown as the best lawman around with the best chance of protecting their money. They held this view ever since cattlemen W.L. Colcord and Andrew Drumm had advised Caldwell leaders to hire Brown in the first place.

On Saturday morning, September 29, Treasurer Milt Bennett, with Henry Brown by his side, left Caldwell on a train headed to Kansas City. When they arrived, Bennett cashed the check and "expressed the money to Muskogee, he and Brown going on the same train."[257]

But when they got to Muskogee, Bennett could find no one to identify him so he could get the cash in silver to deliver to Tahlequah. So Bennett and Brown went to Tahlequah where

"The boys would make excellent constables."

Bennett found Judge George O. Sanders. The three men then headed back to Muskogee. Bennett finally was able to get the cash in silver.

Milt Bennett and Henry Brown now had the most dangerous part of the trip ahead of them. They left Muskogee headed for Tahlequah and hoping no outlaws had caught on to the dangerous journey they were making.

The Caldwell paper said "The distance between the two places is about 35 miles, over a road none the best, and lined on each side with brush a good portion of the distance. Milt says the trip is the most disagreeable one he ever made in his life, and nothing could induce him to repeat the experience. Notwithstanding the assurance he received that the road was perfectly free from all highwaymen or would-be robbers, all the time he was on the road, a suspicion prevailed in his mind that a half dozen men were liable to jump out of the brush at any time and compel him to throw out the grip containing the money."[258]

Marshal Henry Brown had been in a number of dangerous situations before. This one would be just one more of them. But he would never have a better chance to rob a bigger payroll than what he protected that day. Seven months later he would actually carry out an attempt at robbery.

◊

Two of Caldwell's leading lawmen, Deputy U.S. Marshal Cash Hollister and Caldwell Assistant Marshal Ben Wheeler, hauled a dead man to Caldwell on Wednesday, November 21. They explained what happened.

Earlier that day Albert Banks, 16-year-old son of Gerard Banks, who lived about nine miles from Caldwell, came to town with a neighbor, J.W. Loverton. The Banks boy and Loverton swore out a warrant for Chet Van Meter's arrest. Van Meter was Gerard Banks' son-in-law. They said Van Meter beat his wife on Tuesday night, shot at Loverton and a Miss Doty, and next morning beat Albert

153

Banks and threatened to kill a half dozen of those in that neighborhood.

Justice of the Peace T.H.B. Ross deputized Cash Hollister to serve the warrant, asking him to get help and go well armed. Hollister got his shotgun and chose Ben Wheeler. The two lawmen headed to the Banks farm around four p.m. There they learned that Van Meter had just gone to his father's house. The two lawmen rode another five miles.

As the rode up to the farm, they spotted Van Meter standing at the southeast corner of the house with a Winchester at his side. Hollister and Wheeler jumped out of their wagon.

Wheeler called out for Van Meter to hold up his hands. Van Meter raised his arms but then fired at the lawmen. Quickly Hollister and Wheeler fired back. Before Van Meter could fire again, both lawmen fired a second time. Van Meter fell dead in his tracks.

He had bullet holes in his right side, chest, belly, and both hands. A jury ruled that Van Meter died "at the hands of C.M. Hollister and Ben Wheeler while in the discharge of their duties as officers of the law."[259]

◊

Just before Christmas time, on Friday night, December 14, 1883, Brown and Wheeler faced more trouble. It came from a gambler who extended his stay.

Texas gambler Newt Boyce and his wife stayed in Caldwell after the 1883 cattle season. That Friday night Boyce took part in a fight at a saloon on the east side of Main Street. Boyce knifed a soldier and a saloonkeeper. Ben Wheeler soon arrived, took away the knife, and told Boyce to go home.

Later someone came to Brown and Wheeler at the Southwestern Hotel and told them Boyce was on the warpath again. The lawmen found Boyce in Hulbert's store buying a knife and revolver. Brown arrested him.

154

"The boys would make excellent constables."

Next day, Saturday, December 15, Boyce paid a fine and left the jail. Later that day he got drunk and threatened to kill the lawmen. In a saloon north of the post office Wheeler overheard Boyce say he would kill Brown after he'd finished dealing Monte. Wheeler relayed the message to Brown.

Shortly after that Wheeler saw Boyce outside Moore's Saloon. Boyce asked Wheeler where Brown was. Wheeler told him he was in Moore's, but to go home. Boyce and Wheeler then heard footsteps inside the saloon approaching the entrance. Boyce backed into a nearby alley. When Wheeler turned his back, Boyce pulled his gun and aimed it at Wheeler but put it away when he saw another man, T.L. Crist, watching. Boyce quickly left the scene.

Crist told Wheeler what had gone on behind Wheeler's back. As they were still talking, Henry Brown came out of the saloon. Wheeler told Brown the situation. Brown got his Winchester and walked with Wheeler north on the west side of Main Street till they came to H.C. Unsell's Lone Star Clothing House. There they spotted Boyce across the street standing on the sidewalk in front of Phillip's Saloon.

The lawmen started crossing the street. When about 30 feet from Boyce, Brown called out for him to freeze. Boyce ignored Brown's command. He reached in his breast pocket and stepped behind an awning post. Brown leveled his Winchester and fired twice. Boyce ran toward the door of the saloon and fell down just inside. One ball had entered his right arm close to the shoulder and gone in his right side.

Boyce died about three o'clock the next morning. A jury cleared Brown of any wrongdoing.[260]

This action only added to Brown's reputation. A few believed Brown killed Boyce to silence him since he knew something about Brown's unsavory past. But most believed Brown shot in the line of duty and in self-defense. They admired him as a hero who stood for law and order in a town that needed it.

"That they have brought disgrace on the city, no one can help."

Henry Brown, always the outsider, longed to be an equal among Caldwell leaders. They had hired him but he was not one of them. Town leaders were married with families, had roots in town businesses, had substantial savings and comfortable homes admired by others.

Brown had none of these. Single, he lived at the Southwestern Hotel, had no savings, and owned no business. His chances of circulating among the elite seemed remote to nil. But he soon found a way to move a step closer.

On Wednesday, March 26, 1884, "Rev. [Dudley E.] Akin officiated, and in a few quiet remarks joined Mr. Henry N. Brown and Miss [Alice] Maude Levagood in the holy bonds of wedlock."[261] This became the first giant step he made toward his goal. Brown and his 22-year-old wife honeymooned for a week at the Southwestern Hotel.[262]

Early April the new city council again reappointed Brown and Wheeler to their positions. Brown now received $125 a month and Wheeler $100.[263]

Brown took the second step in his move up the ladder. On April 2, he bought a house. "Henry Brown has bought the Robt. Eatock place," said the paper, "and has gone to house-keeping." The house was located six blocks north of the main downtown area. He even bought a milk cow for his wife.[264]

But this left him in debt. He had to start paying off a mortgage on the house. With no savings and no source of a monetary windfall, he found himself behind the eight ball. Other than that it looked like he was on his way up.

Sunday afternoon, April 27, 1884, after a month of married life, Henry Newton Brown rode west out of town with Ben Wheeler. Brown told newly elected Mayor William Morris they were going after a murderer in Indian Territory and would be back in a few days.[265]

The two lawmen rode west that afternoon on their way to Harper. That same afternoon two cowboys, Billy Smith and John Wesley, planned on joining the lawmen. Wesley rode north, met Billy Smith, and the two rode toward the Gypsum Hills south of Medicine Lodge.

Billy Smith, in his late 20s, from Vernon, Texas, worked as the "through herd ramrod" (that is, the Texas cattle herd boss) for the T5 ranch (Texas Land and Cattle Company) in the Cherokee Outlet southwest of Caldwell. He had worked as a T5 horse wrangler till he replaced the Bean brothers as herd boss. (The Bean brothers killed Caldwell Marshal George Brown in June 1882, fled to Texas, were later caught, and died from "lead poisoning").

Smith's friends at the T5 knew he sometimes lived on the wild side. Oliver Nelson, the T5 ranch cook, remembered some of Smith's talk back in December 1882.

"The boys at the line camps worked hard during the storms, but in nice weather they hadn't much to do," he said. "They sat in their dugouts and read up on Wild West history, especially gun men, and figured out the best way to steal Indian ponies and be plumb safe. Once in a get-money talk Billy Smith told how the U.S. paymaster used to come down the Cantone Trail when there was a garrison at the post, and how he and another T5 boy and two from Quinlan's layed out for him, aiming to shoot the guards and make away with the money." The paymaster ended up taking another route and the cowboys left empty-handed.

"That they have brought disgrace on the city, no one can help."

"It was common talk at the west camp that to rob the bank at Medicine Lodge would be an easy job," Nelson added. "I took it all for fun, and in a way it was – just deviltry and love of adventure – but there wasn't a thing those boys wouldn't do. And a prominent member of the Wildcat Pool [Eagle Chief Pool], a treacherous windbag, was interested in the pony stealing and was helping them frame the bank robbery."[266]

John Wesley, about 31, from Paris, Texas, had worked for the Treadwell and Clark ranch south of Caldwell before joining the T5 shortly before riding with the gang headed west. Oliver Nelson said "When the spring [1884] thaw came, life began to show signs of breaking out. [Billy] Smith took on a boy name John Wesley and rode the range."[267]

Next day, Monday, April 28, the two lawmen may have rested in Harper. That day Smith and Wesley left some extra horses in the Gyp Hills near a newly fenced area, at least according to one story. They figured they could use the fence as a landmark to find the fresh mounts after they robbed the bank.

Tuesday, April 29, the four men met in the Gyp Hills. They reviewed plans and made ready for the monetary event. A fifth man planned to watch the extra horses till the four arrived after their mission.

That night Wheeler and Smith stayed with a settler named Ben Harbaugh. He lived eight miles south of Medicine Lodge and two or three east of the Gyp Hills. Brown and Wesley stayed in the Hills.

Wednesday morning, April 30, clouds filled the sky. Rain fell. The four men rode north to Medicine Lodge, entering from the west a little after nine a.m. They carried 44 caliber revolvers and Winchester rifles.

They tied their horses behind the Medicine Valley Bank. Billy Smith stayed with the horses while the others headed for money. Brown and Wesley entered the bank's side door while Wheeler entered the front.

As luck would have it, a group of cowboys happened to be holed up in a livery stable across the street. They were waiting for the rain to let up before going on a roundup at Antelope Flat.

Inside the bank Wesley looked for any unwanted customers, then guarded the side entrance. Brown walked up to bank president Edward Wylie Payne and called for him to raise his hands. Wheeler covered cashier George Geppert.

Bank president Payne, 36, helped organize the Cherokee Strip Live Stock Association, controlled the 45-mile square Comanche Pool with more than 50,000 cattle, and held thousands of his own cattle around Medicine Lodge. People respected and admired him. He had a wife and nine children. Cashier Geppert, 41, also worked as a partner in a hardware and lumber store. He also was married and had one son.

Payne grabbed for his pistol. Brown drilled him with a .44. Geppert raised his hands and turned his head toward Payne. Wheeler shot Geppert with a .44. Then Wheeler or Wesley shot Geppert a second time.

Geppert struggled to lock the vault before falling over dead. Payne groaned on the floor, mortally wounded. He died next day, but lived long enough to finger Brown and Wheeler as the shooters.

Outside, shots startled citizens. Marshal Sam Denn saw Billy Smith standing by the horses. Denn pulled his gun and shot. Smith shot back. Neither hit their target.

The outlaws ran out of the bank to their horses, struggled to loosen the wet reins, and retreated south toward the Gyp Hills. The cowboys in the livery stable soon followed in hot pursuit.

The outlaws had two strikes against them. Wheeler's horse pulled up lame, slowing them down. Then the outlaws couldn't find their reserve horses. One story said a farmer had worked on the landmark fence, extending it to a different place.

As rain poured down, Henry Brown mistakenly led his men into a small blind canyon, later known as Jackass Canyon, about 5 ½ miles south and 1 ¼ miles west of Medicine Lodge. The canyon had only one way in and out. The pursuers quickly covered the

"That they have brought disgrace on the city, no one can help."

entrance as the outlaws went deeper inside. Rainwater began filling the canyon till the outlaws found themselves in a foot and a half to two feet of it.

They held out for two hours. With water rising and no hope of escape, Henry Brown decided to give up, though Billy Smith didn't want to. Smith figured they would be signing their death warrant.

The posse brought the four outlaws back to Medicine Lodge. They cuffed Brown's right ankle to Wesley's left and Wheeler's right wrist to Smith's left. The lawmen took the four outlaws to the town café for lunch before taking them to jail. The rain stopped.

A photographer happened to be at the jail when the men arrived. He took a picture that showed the four outlaws in front of the wooden jail surrounded by a crowd of citizens. Then Barber County Sheriff C.T. Rigg put the four inside.

Barber County Attorney Joe McNeal questioned the outlaws while they were in jail. He hoped to prepare for their trial and needed information about their actions. Years later he revealed testimony from Ben Wheeler, who spoke about a plot between Wheeler and cashier George Geppert. According to what Wheeler told McNeal, Geppert owed money to the bank and hoped to hide the debt through the planned bank robbery.[268]

The outlaws spent the rest of day there. Henry Newton Brown wrote a letter to his wife in Caldwell. In it he anticipated deadly consequences. "I will send you all of my things, and you can sell them, but keep the Winchester," he said. He ended the letter saying "If a mob does not kill us we will come out all right after while. Maude, I did not shoot any one, and did not want the others to kill any one but they did, and that is all there is about it. Now, good-bye, my darling wife."[269]

Wesley worked his way out of his leg iron, and Smith, out of his handcuff. Around nine p.m. three shots pierced through the night air. About 300 men surrounded the jail and forced the sheriff and posse to give up the prisoners.

When the mob opened the door, Henry Brown leaped out and ran, followed by random shots. He got to an alley east of the jail before a farmer, Billy Kelley, blasted him with a shotgun. He died instantly. Others fired into his body.

Wheeler tried to run another direction when a fusillade of bullets struck him. One clipped off one of his fingers. Others slammed into his back and right arm. He still struggled to run, but the mob caught him.

The crowd took him, Wesley, and Smith to a large elm tree a few hundred yards east of the jail. There they left them hanging in the breeze.

The first notice Caldwell received about the Medicine Lodge incident came Thursday morning though with few details. Caldwell leader Ben S. Miller received a telegram around 6:30 p.m. that day from Medicine Lodge Mayor Charles E. Eldred filling in some details.

"The bank robbers were Brown and Wheeler, marshal and deputy of Caldwell, and Smith and Wesley," it said. "All arrested. Tried to escape. Brown killed. Balance hung. Geppert dead. Payne will die."[270]

At first citizens refused to believe the report. They figured Medicine Lodge made a mistake. How could the two best lawmen Caldwell ever had be involved in an attempted bank robbery and murder? But shocked belief set in as Caldwell citizens read the May 1 and May 8 *Medicine Lodge Cresset* which listed Brown and Wheeler among the outlaws.

Caldwell felt embarrassed and apologetic for Brown and Wheeler's behavior. Delegates representing the town traveled to Medicine Lodge and expressed their sympathy for the friends and relatives of the victims. The Caldwell paper expressed the town's feelings about the matter, saying "That they [Brown and Wheeler] have brought disgrace on the city, no one can help; and that they met their just deserts, all rejoice."[271]

Oliver Nelson said his brother Charles went to Medicine Lodge to put a claim on the money Billy Smith owed them. When he did, the judge and sheriff insulted Charles. Smith rode a good Kentucky mare. Two of the other horses were worth plenty.

162

"The [the four outlaws] had four good saddles, four rifles, four pistols, and about $3,000," said Nelson. "But something happened to their money; not enough cash showed up to pay the grave digger."[272]

Henry Brown's wife, Alice Maud along with relative Newt Miller, soon went to Medicine Lodge and brought back the body, according to several accounts. Caldwell historian Rod Cook believed Henry was later buried in the Caldwell cemetery at a plot owned by Levi Thraillkill. However, when Thrailkill's unmarked plots were dug up to confirm this, the investigators found no body.[273]

◊

On Monday, May 5, 1884, Mayor William Morris appointed John Phillips as the new town marshal to replace Henry Brown. Phillips chose policeman Bedford B. Wood as his assistant to replace Ben Wheeler.

This came three years and a month after Phillips was first appointed marshal. That time he quit because the city council lowered the marshal's salary. This time he reaped the benefit of Marshal Brown's inflated salary.

Phillips and Wood's service as the city's chief lawmen pleased Caldwell residents. They kept the cowboys on a tight leash but didn't interfere with business. During the busy season they made more than 150 arrests. Most were for minor charges such as disorderly conduct while drunk, prostitution, gambling. Income from these arrests boosted the city treasury while allowing cowboys some leeway.

◊

Friday night, October 17, around 11 p.m. lawman Cash Hollister, who resigned as deputy U.S. marshal five weeks earlier but had been serving as Sumner County deputy sheriff since February, left

Caldwell for Hunnewell to serve a warrant. The 38-year-old lawman took two others with him; George Davis and Joshua Hannum, who swore out the warrant.

Hannum claimed Bob Cross, a Texas cowboy, abducted his daughter. Cross also had two other warrants against him. Hannum said Cross kidnapped his daughter and took her to Cedar Vale in Chatauqua County on Sunday, October 12.

On Thursday, October 16, Cross returned with her to Wellington and that night put her on a train to Caldwell promising to meet her there on Friday morning. Hannum's daughter figured out Cross had abandoned her so she returned home.

Cross instead picked up his wife in Bluff Township on Friday and the two went to his brother-in-law Fin Warrenburg's place one mile north and two east of Hunnewell. Somehow Deputy Sheriff Hollister heard that Cross was at T.M. Warrenburg's place near Hunnewell. That's when he, Davis, and Hannum headed toward Hunnewell.

At Hunnewell Hollister looked up town marshal Reilly, who agreed to go with them. The four arrived at the Warrenburg house about three a.m. Joshua Hannum stayed with the wagon while the other three surrounded the house.

One of the men called out for Cross to surrender. A woman inside answered. She swore Cross was not there. The men kicked the door open. They asked for a lamp to see inside. The woman refused, then slammed the door. The men kicked it open again.

Two shots from a Winchester blasted through the doorway from inside. Neither found their mark. The lawmen jumped back, then threatened to burn the house down. Women came out but not Cross.

George Davis started stuffing hay under the house when another shot came from inside. Hollister dropped to the ground at the southwest corner. Davis ran behind a woodpile. Marshal Reilly stood at the northeast corner guarding two windows.

Davis crawled to Hollister and was surprised to discover he lay dead from the last shot. Reilly wanted Davis to guard the door, but

Davis insisted on taking Hollister back to Hunnewell. When he tried, though, he scared off the horses.

While Davis went to retrieve the horses and wagon, Reilly watched Mrs. Cross enter the house. She came out standing between Bob Cross and Marshal Reilly. Reilly raised his gun.

Mrs. Cross sprang toward Reilly, grabbed hold of the gun and kept it aimed at herself. Reilly jerked it away and again tried to aim at Cross. Mrs. Cross again grabbed the gun. Cross, who had nothing but his shirt on, leaped away and ran into the darkness.

Davis finally got control of the horse team and loaded Hollister in the wagon. He arrested the women and took them in the wagon along with Hollister's body to Hunnewell. Someone telephoned Caldwell Mayor Morris, who came to Hunnewell.

At Hunnewell the lawmen got a fresh team to haul Hollister and the prisoners back to Caldwell. The group arrived in town around 10:30 that morning.

A party led by Bedford Wood and Marshal Reilly found Bob Cross "lying flat on the ground in a little draw" by Bluff Creek around four p.m. that same day. The lawmen took Cross to Hunnewell and kept him closely guarded before heading on to Wellington.

"It was well they started when they did," said the Caldwell paper, "or his [Cross's] body would have been found hanging to a telegraph pole the next morning."[274]

◊

Though Caldwell Marshal John Phillips protected the town through the 1884 cattle season efficiently, his greatest challenge came later. It happened at 6 p.m. on Saturday, November 15.

Cowboy Oscar Thomas, who worked for the Washita Cattle Company, came to Caldwell a week or so earlier wanting to exercise his freedom and enjoy himself in his time off. To do that, he carried a dirk knife and usually one or two six-shooters.

Caldwell by then had a city ordinance against carrying a gun, so Thomas' friends tried to get him to leave his weapons behind when celebrating in town. But Thomas swore he would kill anyone who tried to take his guns from him. In fact, he claimed he would rather die than give them up. This reflected the attitude of a number of cowboys.

Day after day his behavior while drinking got worse. It finally reached the breaking point. Even his friends couldn't figure out what he would do next. They told Marshal Phillips to be on guard. Phillips tried to get Thomas to leave town without trouble, but Thomas refused.

What made things worse, Oscar Thomas had a grudge against the A. Witzleben and B.W. Key mercantile store, which had replaced York, Parker, and Drake. The store turned down his request to buy goods on credit. So Thomas returned to the store repeatedly and to argue with the clerk, Mack Killibraw.

That Saturday evening, November 15, Killibraw took all the abuse he figured he could handle. This time when Thomas berated him, Killibraw grabbed an ax and got ready to use it before Witzleben snatched it out of Killibraw's hands. This gave Thomas a chance to make a move. Thomas drew his gun, but Killibraw seized the moment. He grabbed hold of the .45. Right then Marshal Phillips appeared on the scene.

Phillips drew his .45. "Throw up your hands!" he told Thomas.

The cowboy turned toward Phillips, leaving his hands at his side. "Throw up your hands!" Phillips repeated. Thomas, instead, reached for his gun. Phillips fired. Thomas fell behind a counter.

Assistant Marshal Bedford Wood then entered the side door. Phillips ordered Thomas to throw up his hands a third time. Thomas refused. Phillips yelled to Wood to shoot Thomas. Wood fired his .45. The ball hit Thomas in the head. He fell to the floor. The lawmen took a .45-caliber six-shooter and a four-inch dirk knife from him.

Doctors found two wounds in Thomas: the first through the left side of his chest that came out the right side of his spinal column, the second through the back of his head that came out through his forehead. The lawmen took Thomas to the city jail, where he died at nine a.m. Sunday, November 16.

Jurors ruled that the lawmen's behavior in shooting Thomas was "justifiable and commendable and that said officers were acting in the line of their duty as officers of the city of Caldwell and in a careful and prudent manner."[275]

◊

Most people in and around Caldwell knew its days as a cattle-shipping center were coming to an end. Farmers and homesteaders were glad it was. Merchants had mixed feelings. They liked the business. They could only hope something else would take up the slack when cowboys and cattle left.

"Thus is added another victim killed by unknown parties."

People in and around Caldwell knew the town was changing by 1884. Saloons saw fewer cowboys, especially those from Texas. Farmers were replacing them as they shopped for implements and feed. All land around town was fenced in.

More talk about prohibition filled the streets. Though prohibition had become Kansas law in 1880, saloons continued to serve liquor freely. Town leaders collected fines from these businesses rather than jailing the owners. But now things were changing. Strong prohibition backers carried the day. People were ready to crack down on this illegal activity.

Winter, 1884-85 also proved to be a bad omen for Caldwell's future as a cow town. Cowboy Oliver Nelson described that winter as he experienced it around his homestead west of Caldwell. He remembered the ground froze three inches deep before snow came on December 17. That day it snowed five inches. "It just kept snowing about once a week," he said.

"The cattle were fat in November. With the snow they came to low ground. It rained twice between Christmas and New Year's, then snowed and froze. Six inches of ice covered the ground, then more snow on top. Sometimes a ball of ice would form on a cow's nose – a ball five inches across, with two small holes made for breathing. The poor things just walked the creeks and bawled. The mercury got down to 17 below. In February their feet, and then their legs froze. When it would turn warm, the legs would break at the ankle or knee. Sometimes they would rest on the pegs a day or so before they would lay down. When down, they could not get up. They died by thousands."[276]

In 1885, Caldwell cattle shipments dropped to less than a third of what they were in 1884. Citizens saw a number of reasons besides bad weather.

Barbed wire fences proliferated. South of Caldwell where cattlemen had joined together to form the Cherokee Strip Live Stock Association in 1883 each ranch fenced in its own area.

The country surrounding Caldwell and to the north had filled up with settlers. Farmers and cattlemen owned and fenced in most of that land. Open range became increasingly rare.

Quarantine laws had closed down the Chisholm Trail in Kansas back in 1875. Some Texas cattlemen refused to give up. Between 1883 and 1885 they pressed for Congress to open a National Trail. They proposed a path along the eastern edge of Colorado. But it never happened.[277]

Cattlemen increasingly bred domestic stock. Demand for Texas cattle continued to drop as cattle herds multiplied in the midwestern, western, and northern states.

Texas railroads lowered their rates and competed more aggressively for the Texas cattle. This made it cheaper for Texas cattlemen to ship their herds to eastern cities than to drive them to Caldwell.

Cattlemen in the Caldwell area felt the land around there should feed livestock. Homesteaders thought it should grow crops. The Cherokee Outlet south of Caldwell continued to be a battleground among these groups.

These groups had battled ever since Caldwell had become a railhead. And it heated up as each year went by.

In the early years, cattlemen had the advantage. They fattened their stock on rich grass in the Cherokee Outlet south, ignoring U.S. law against occupying Indian land. But the Cherokees didn't live on this land they owned. And that gave them the opening they needed, as was discussed in an earlier chapter.

Ever since the CSLSA had become an official organization in 1883, a number of homesteaders strongly opposed them. These bitter opponents gradually became better organized as they pointed out how unfair it was to allow cattlemen in an area closed to them.

That's how the most famous leader of the homesteaders, Captain David L. Payne, who vociferously challenged the ranchers' right to be in the Outlet, increased his following. His argument made ever more sense as the years passed.

Payne questioned the legality of ranchers in the Cherokee Outlet ever since they had settled there. His own view had taken shape in 1879. That year he saw even more clearly why he believed homesteaders had a right to settle in Oklahoma. He even based it on the treaty of 1866. He believed that treaty made this land a part of the public domain. To him, that meant United States citizens had the right to settle there.

Payne soon organized colonies of homesteaders eager to stake their claims. These colonies continued to attract others as they traveled across southern border towns in Kansas. In December 1880 Payne stirred up enthusiasts in Arkansas City, Hunnewell, and Caldwell.

Throughout the 1880s Payne repeatedly tried to establish homesteads in Oklahoma. Each time government troops stopped him. His followers became known as "boomers." Whether arrested and jailed, or simply forced to return to Kansas, boomers continued to move into Oklahoma. By the middle 80s public sentiment began to switch heavily in favor of the boomers. Ranchers realized their time was running out.

Major Gordon W. "Pawnee Bill" Lillie found himself in the middle of this conflict in 1883 when he went to Caldwell. By then he had more sympathy for the boomers.

At that time he worked for the Zimmerman Ranch in the Cherokee Outlet. He went to Caldwell that year on a cattle drive with Major Zimmerman. When Lillie and Zimmerman first rode into Caldwell, they noticed farmers camped outside the town in wagons. Banners on the wagons read, "Strike for a home," "No turn back," "Uncle Sam is rich enough; Give us all a home in Oklahoma," and more. Zimmerman and Lillie soon got in an argument about the boomers, Zimmerman against and Lillie for.

The more Lillie found out about Payne, the more he agreed with him. Lillie read Payne's paper, the *War Chief*, and became convinced Payne stood for a good cause. Lillie decided to quit his job on the cattle range. He hired on as a waiter in Caldwell.

He expressed his opinions in town and soon got Payne's attention. One day Payne ordered breakfast where Lillie worked as a waiter. Payne soon struck up a conversation with Lillie and suggested he lead a colony of boomers.

In June 1880 went to Payne's headquarters in Geuda Springs to join a colony, but Payne at that time lay bedridden and cancelled a plan to move into Indian Territory in July. So instead of joining a colony, Lillie joined a Wild West show similar to Buffalo Bill's.[278] From then on, though, Lillie championed the boomers' cause.

The conflict between boomers and cattleman was bound to affect the future of Caldwell. Cowboys and cattlemen still made up much of Caldwell's business, especially during the spring and summer. Yet farmers and homesteaders also supported the town and they sympathized with boomers.

This battle continued till boomers triumphed in 1889 when the government allowed them to settle in Oklahoma. This put the final nail in Caldwell's coffin as a cattle town.

The 1885 season, unlike past years, saw no major gun battles in Caldwell. With dying numbers of "through herds," the town experienced far fewer celebrating Texas cowboys.

One cowboy who started a Caldwell business in 1884 found a new source of success. Charlie Siringo, who had chased Billy the Kid and Henry Newton Brown before locating in Caldwell, used the 1884 Medicine Lodge bank holdup to launch his new career as an author.

Shortly after Brown and his three companions bit the dust in Medicine Lodge, Siringo wrote newspaper articles about his experience chasing the outlaws and working as a cowboy. In 1885

172

he completed a book on his experiences, called *A Texas Cowboy or Fifteen Years on the Hurricane Deck of a Spanish Pony.*

Conflicts in the 1880s erupted not only between boomers and cattlemen. Another issue that stirred up trouble centered on the conflict between prohibitionists and saloonkeepers.

The prohibition issue created as much trouble as did the boomers in 1885. Though Caldwell up till then hadn't enforced the state's prohibition law, the tide began to turn as saloon business dropped. With fewer cowboys in town and less alcohol consumed, merchants had fewer motives to buck the law.

Town leaders paid more attention to protests from citizens. Prohibition forces grew stronger. The prohibition issue and illegal alcohol trade, one way or another, may have been behind another killing in Caldwell near the end of 1885.

At 2:30 a.m. on Monday, August 31, 1885 neighbors of Enos Blair noticed his house burning. They rushed inside, woke Blair, and led him outside. Citizens extinguished the fire before it could damage the furniture inside. They felt lucky.

But when residents figured out how the fire started, they burned with anger. Someone deliberately started it with a ball of candle wicking soaked in oil.[279]

Why someone would do this to one of Caldwell's pioneer settlers remained a question. Blair, a livestock dealer, also edited and published the *Caldwell Free Press* at the time.

In the brief time this paper existed, Blair espoused prohibition and editorialized against lawlessness in the city, whether it involved drinking, gambling, prostitution, or general disorderly conduct displayed by cowboys on the rampage. Citizens came up with several suspects.

Many believed cowboys had something to do with the burning. But no one could prove this. Two other suspects, Frank Noyes and Dave Sharp, had served 30 days in jail the previous August for illegal liquor sales, and were released before Enos Blair's house burned.

More than three months went by. Then early Tuesday morning, December 8, a dray driver riding by shipping pens near the Caldwell Santa Fe train station looked up at the frame above one of the gates.

There a man dangled from a rope.

Soon a crowd gathered. Several recognized the victim as Frank Noyes, the Caldwell gambler who along with Dave Sharp had served jail time. Someone found a note in Noyes' shirt pocket. It said he was hanged for house burning.[280]

An early arrival at the scene, George Gentry, found a glove near Noyes' body with a name on it. The paper never revealed the name. On December 17 two men, Jesse Lambert and Dan W. Jones, one of the lawman accused of killing George Flatt, were tried for the lynching.

Noyes' girlfriend, May "Mamie" Fernie, testified against Lambert and Jones. She claimed to recognize both men on the night men took Noyes away. The *Sumner County Press* added fuel to the fire when it described Jones as a "desperado."[281]

Jones became highly offended at the paper's description of him and wrote a rebuttal the following week. In it he listed numerous leading citizens who knew him to be an honest and conscientious lawman throughout his career. However, in his rebuttal he did admit to having a wild streak, as did another apologist for him.[282] In the end both men were acquitted.

So again a jury found no perpetrator or the crime. "Thus is added another victim, killed by unknown parties," said George Freeman.[283]

This didn't stop residents from forming numerous theories on who lynched Noyes. A number of stories had validity.

Several fires happened around the time Blair's house burned. On July 7 Kelpatrick and Yorke's implement warehouse burned. On August 16 Griffith and Swartzel's stable and granary burned. On September 27 a building near the City Hotel burned. On October 3 the same building burned down. On October 8 the City Hotel burned down. Cause for all these fires remained a mystery.

"Thus is added another victim killed by unknown parties."

So Noyes' killers may have simply thought he started the fires and should die for that.

Two factions in town that had some of the strongest feelings against each other were the law and order prohibition group and merchants who hoped for continuing business from drinkers. Prohibitionists, some thought, had good reason to hang gambler Noyes, who had been convicted of dealing in illegal alcohol.

George Freeman mentioned that Noyes had just won several hundred dollars gambling before being killed. Some thought Noyes' fellow gamblers killed him for the money.

Whatever stood behind the lynching, it showed Caldwell citizens still believed shortcut justice worked. Freeman's take on Caldwell seemed the right one. The town still thought justice delayed was justice denied. But this view was slowly dying out, as was Caldwell as a cow town.

◊

Caldwell's days as a cow town soon became past tense. But what it brought to the American way of life didn't.

In at least a couple of ways early Caldwell had a lasting effect. For one thing, Caldwell, along with the other cow towns, played a crucial role in changing America's eating habits.

Texas cattle drives, a large part traveling the Chisholm Trail going through Caldwell, opened a whole new national market. McDonald's Restaurants became one of its greatest beneficiaries.

Before the Civil War, cattle used for beef mainly centered in the eastern third of the -United States, plus Texas and California. The rest of the North and West had next to none. By 1880 cattlemen had spread throughout the country. As a result, between 1860 and 1880 the price of beef dropped to make it the preferred meat of the common man as well as the millionaire in America.

"The open-range and range-ranching phases of the Great Plains economy had served American consumers well," said historian Frederick Merk. "They had contributed abundant quantities of beef to the market at reduced prices, so that meat came within the reach of workers in the cities."[284]

For another thing, Caldwell and other cow towns gave America a new hero, the cowboy. Scholars have argued about why people like cowboys, how much of the image comes from history and how much from fiction, and exactly how the image grew from negative to positive. But few would disagree that the cowboy has since played a major role in America's life.

No town experienced more cowboys coming and going than did Caldwell. They came from cattle drives headed north on the Chisholm Trail and passing through the Caldwell gateway to Kansas in the late 60s. They came from ranches in the Cherokee Outlet in the 70s and 80s. They came from cattlemen and old cowboys such as Charlie Siringo who lived in Caldwell.

Today the size of Caldwell remains nearly the same as it was during its cow town days. And with help from a number of historical markers constructed throughout the town in 1993, it's not impossible to imagine what this place might have been like back then.[285] The role it played in American history should not be underestimated.

Footnotes

Introduction

[1] Bill O'Neal, *Caldwell in the 1870s and 1880s: The Rowdy Years of the Border Queen* (self published, no date), 17.

[2] Ray Allen Billington and Martin Ridge, *Westward Expansion: A History of the American Frontier*, 5th Edition (New York: MacMillan Publishing Co., Inc., 1982), 645-646.

Chapter 1 – "Uncle Sam, at that time, had plenty of land."

[3] William G. Cutler, *History of the State of Kansas* (Chicago: A.T. Andreas, 1883), Sumner County, Part 9.

[4] H. Craig Miner, *Wichita: The Early Years, 1865-80* (Lincoln: University of Nebraska Press, 1982), 33.

[5] William Frank Zornow, *Kansas: A History of the Jayhawk State* (Norman: University of Oklahoma Press, 1957), 149.

[6] Ibid., 150.

[7] John P. Edwards, *Historical Atlas of Sumner County, Kansas* (Philadelphia, 1883), 7.

[8] William G. Cutler, *History of the State of Kansas* (Chicago: A.T. Andreas, 1883), Sumner County, Part 7 and Caldwell Messenger, September 3, 1953.

[9] *Caldwell Messenger*, September 3, 1953. See also Cutler's *History* and John P. Edwards' *Historical Atlas of Sumner County*. The *Emporia News*, February 17, 1871 said "The last sensation in the way of a city is that of the new town of Caldwell, recently laid off in Sumner County. It is located near Fall River at the crossing

of the Texas cattle trail. The town company is principally composed of Southwestern Kansas men. Wm. Baldwin is president, C. F. Gilbert treasurer, and G. H. Smith, secretary." The *Wichita Vidette*, February 25, 1871 said "Judge Baldwin is president of the company and G. I. Smith esq., secretary." It is unclear why the Emporia and Wichita lists of officers differed from Caldwell's, and why neither mentioned Stone. William Baldwin settled east of Wichita in 1870. In the spring of 1872 he became city attorney of Wichita. In 1877 through 1878 he served as a Sedgwick County representative. He may have helped form the Caldwell Town Company, then relinquished leadership to Charles Gilbert by March 1871.

[10] So did the authors of the early historical accounts of Caldwell. Neither Cutler's *History of the State of Kansas* (1883) nor William E. Connelley's *A Standard History of Kansas and Kansans* (1918) mentioned anything negative about Caldwell. Cutler said Caldwell "resigned his position to give his attention to business interests which were being neglected." Connelley said he resigned "his exalted position to attend to a multiplicity of other duties." Later historians have not been so kind. Robert W. Richmond, in *Kansas: A Land of Contrasts* (1974) said "it was thought that Caldwell reached the Senate because he paid the right people." Kenneth S. Davis, in *Kansas: A History* (1984) said "Alexander Caldwell . . . bought the election for $60,000."

[11] *Caldwell Journal*, January 1, 1885.

[12] The *WPA Guide to 1930s Kansas* (Lawrence: University Press of Kansas, 1984, originally published, 1939), pp. 462-463, and *Caldwell Messenger*, September 3, 1953.

[13] *Caldwell Messenger*, September 3, 1953, and G.D. Freeman in *Midnight and Noonday* (Norman: University of Oklahoma Press, 1984), 32.

[14] G.D. Freeman, *Midnight and Noonday* (Norman: University of Oklahoma Press, 1984), 80-81.

[15] *Ibid.*, 81.

[16] When the *Emporia News*, February 17, 1871, wrote about the new town of Caldwell, it ended the article with an appeal, saying,

"There will be three stores opened immediately, also one hotel and a
livery stable. Liberal inducements are offered to a first-class
blacksmith. For information address G. H. Smith, Wichita."
[17] G.D. Freeman, *Midnight and Noonday* (Norman: University of
Oklahoma Press, 1984), 24.
[18] *Ibid.*, 23.
[19] William G. Cutler, *History of the State of Kansas* (Chicago:
A.T. Andreas, 1883), "Sumner County, Part 7."
[20] Mrs. J.B. Rideout, *Six Years On The Border* (Philadelphia:
Presbyterian Board of Publication, 1883); quoted in Donald White,
The Border Queen: A History of Early Day Caldwell, Kansas
(Wyandotte, Oklahoma: The Gregath Publishing, 1999), 271.

Chapter 2 – Vigilantes on the Rampage

[21] G.D. Freeman, *Midnight and Noonday* (Norman: University of
Oklahoma Press, 1984), 37-39. The *Oxford Times*, Thursday, June
22, 1871, ran an article titled "Indian Outrage" which said "We are
reliably informed that a man named 'Dutch Fred,' living on Bluff
Creek, about forty miles from here, was murdered by a party of
Osages a short time since. It is said he owned a ranch and had been
in the habit of selling liquor to the Indians, and some trouble had
occurred between him and this tribe. He was found with four
arrows in him and two wounds from pistol shots. Life was not
extinct, but his recovery was deemed impossible." News had a way
of changing as distance from the event increased.
[22] John Wesley Hardin, *The Life of John Wesley Hardin as
Written by Himself* (Norman: University of Oklahoma Press, 1961),
35-36.
[23] The *Oxford Times*, July 13, 1871, reported a similar or the
same incident with different details than those of Hardin. The paper
said Cohron's brother killed Bideno in the Southwestern Hotel at
Sumner City, a few miles northwest of Wellington. Hardin said it
happened in Bluff City near the southern border of Kansas.
Problem is, there was no Bluff City at that time. See the "Early

History" of Harper County in William G. Cutler's *History of the State of Kansas* (Chicago: A.T. Andreas, 1883) for an account of a fictitious town by that name. Hardin also said the killing happened in June. More than likely Hardin did kill Bideno, since the *Abilene Chronicle*, August 17, 1871, mentioned that the same person who shot Bideno shot Charles Couger on August 6. And Hardin was the one who shot Couger. See Joseph G. Rosa's *They Called Him Wild Bill* (Norman: University of Oklahoma Press, 1974), 186-187. This incident serves as an example of what it was like to live near the Chisholm Trail at that time.

[24] G.D. Freeman, *Midnight and Noonday* (Norman: University of Oklahoma Press, 1984), 45-48.

[25] *Oxford Times*, September 30, 1871.

[26] G.D. Freeman, *Midnight and Noonday* (Norman: University of Oklahoma Press, 1984), 179-180.

[27] *Ibid.*, 56-59.

[28] *Ibid.*, 72-75.

[29] *Ibid.*, 76-86.

[30] *Topeka Daily Commonwealth*, May 8, 1872. For accounts of the Lynch killing, see *Wellington Monitor Press*, October 14, 1914 and *When Kansas was Young* by Tom A. McNeal (New York: The Macmillan Company), 5.

Chapter 3 – "It was the last chance to get a drink."

[31] G.D. Freeman, *Midnight and Noonday* (Norman: University of Oklahoma Press, 1984), 97-101. Freeman said 35 men were in the posse. The *Wichita Eagle*, June 14, 1872 said there were 18.

[32] G.D. Freeman, *Midnight and Noonday* (Norman: University of Oklahoma Press, 1984), 106.

[33] Tom Smith's real name was Thomas Gord Ford, youngest son of one time Illinois Governor and Supreme Court Justice Thomas Ford (1800-1850). Thomas C. Moore of Peoria, Illinois later adopted him. His older brother was George S. or Sewell Ford (alias Charlie Smith), who ran a trail ranch on the Ninnescah (near present

day Clearwater) before moving south and living near Caldwell, where he caused trouble for George Freeman. See *Sumner County Press*, July 29, 1875, for more background on the Fords. As for Dalton, some have speculated he might have been a member of the famous Dalton brothers who held up two banks in Coffeyville. If he were, he would have been either Charles Benjamin "Ben" Dalton (born February 24, 1852 in Jackson County, Missouri, died March 11, 1936 in Supply, Oklahoma) or Henry Coleman Dalton (born November 26, 1853 in Jackson County, Missouri, died February 28, 1920 in Des Moines, New Mexico).

[34] *Caldwell News*, April 29, 1920.

[35] *Ibid.*, April 1, 1920.

[36] *Ibid.*, April 29, 1920.

[37] G.D. Freeman, *Midnight and Noonday* (Norman: University of Oklahoma Press, 1984), chapter 16 through 19. The *Wichita Eagle*, July 14, 1872, told of the incident in a short article and asked the question of its effect. "The question is, will the farmer have to plow hereafter with a shot-gun looped to the beam and a Navy swung to his side, or not?"

[38] *Caldwell News*, April 15, 1920.

[39] *Wellington Banner*, September 25, 1872.

[40] See *Sumner County Press*, April 23, 1874 and May 7, 1874 issues.

[41] G.D. Freeman, *Midnight and Noonday* (Norman: University of Oklahoma Press, 1984), 93-95. Two other accounts may or may not refer to the same event. The *Topeka Commonwealth*, July 9, 1872 said "Two Texas men renewed an old quarrel at Caldwell on Saturday last, after drinking pretty freely. In the race for the first draw one got his bullet the quickest. The wounded man was shot in the bowels and is reported fatally hurt." The *Wellington Banner*, October 16, 1872, said Frank Moore and James Harris killed each other in Caldwell. The Topeka paper said only one man was shot and had not yet died while the Wellington paper had a much later date for the incident.

[42] *Wichita Eagle*, August 2, 1872.

[43] William G. Cutler, *History of the State of Kansas* (Chicago: A.T. Andreas, 1883), Sumner County, Part 7.

[44] *Wichita Eagle*, May 1, 1873.

[45] *Sumner County Press*, October 9, 1873.

[46] *Ibid.*, November 6, 1873.

[47] *Wichita Eagle*, May 1, 1873.

Chapter 4 – The Indian excitement involves the interest of the state."

[48] *Sumner County Press*, March 5, 1874.

[49] *Wichita Eagle*, March 26, 1874.

[50] Wayne Gard, *The Great Buffalo Hunt* (Lincoln: University of Nebraska Press, 1959), 132.

[51] For more details on the second Adobe Walls fight, see *Great Western Indian Fights* (Lincoln: University of Nebraska Press, 1960), 201-213. This incident and surrounding circumstances led to the Red River War for the next two years. See Robert M. Utley, *Frontier Regulars* (Lincoln: University of Nebraska Press, 1973), 213-235.

[52] *Sumner County Press*, July 2, 1874.

[53] *Topeka Commonwealth*, July 8, 1874.

[54] *Wellington Press*, July 9, 1874.

[55] *Topeka Commonwealth*, Sunday, August 9, 1874.

[56] *Ibid.*, Friday, July 17, 1874.

[57] *Ibid.*, Friday, July 10, 1874. July 7 dispatch from Arkansas City.

[58] *Ibid.*, Friday, July 17, 1874.

[59] Bill O'Neal, *Encyclopedia of Western Gunfighters* (Norman: University of Oklahoma Press, 1979), 47-48.

[60] T.A. McNeal, *When Kansas Was Young* (Topeka: Cappers Publications, Inc., 1940, first published, 1922), 5.

[61] *Wellington Monitor-Press*, August 24, 1924. William Hackney, Joe Thralls, and C.S. Brodbent each had an article in this edition, all of them reminiscing about the excitement in 1874.

[62] *Ibid.*, "Wm. Hackney, Pioneer, Tells of Frontier Life."

[63] *Ibid.*, "An Early Comer to the New Town."

[64] *Topeka Commonwealth*, Tuesday, July 14, 1874, Dispatch from Wichita, July 11.

[65] *Sumner County Press*, July 30, 1874.

[66] *Ibid.*, June 25, 1874, Report from Caldwell.

[67] *Ibid.*, July 2, 1874, Report from Caldwell.

Chapter 5 – "His feet were swaying to and fro."

[68] Richard L. Lane believed George Freeman mistakenly named Neal instead of Thomas C. Gatliff. Both men lived in Wellington, though T.C. usually took an active part in law enforcement. See *Midnight and Noonday*, footnote 13, page 162-163, and the 1884 Wellington City Directory. The July 30, 1874 *Sumner County Press* also mentioned Thomas C. Gatliff by name.

[69] *Sumner County Press*, July 30, 1874.

[70] George D. Freeman, *Midnight and Noonday* (Norman: University of Oklahoma Press, 1984), 175, and Sumner County Press, July 30, 1874.

[71] Mrs. J.B. Rideout, *Six Years on the Border* (Philadelphia: Presbyterian Board of Publication, 1883), quoted in Donald White, *The Border Queen: A History of Early Day Caldwell, Kansas* (Wyandotte, Oklahoma: The Gregath Publishing Company, 1999), 282.

[72] *Belle Plaine Democrat*, Friday, August 22, 1873.

[73] *Sumner County Press*, June 25, 1874.

[74] Mrs. J.B. Rideout, *Six Years on the Border* (Philadelphia: Presbyterian Board of Publication, 1883), quoted in Donald White, *The Border Queen: A History of Early Day Caldwell, Kansas* (Wyandotte, Oklahoma: The Gregath Publishing Company, 1999), 282-283.

[75] *Ibid.*, 282.

[76] G.D. Freeman, *Midnight and Noonday* (Norman, University of Oklahoma Press, 1984), 171. Mrs. Jacob B. Rideout also described

Calkins as a "hotel keeper, a very bad man. His wife was a very bad woman." See Donald White, *The Border Queen: A History of Early Day Caldwell, Kansas* (Wyandotte, Oklahoma: The Gregath Publishing Company, 1999), 282.

[77] George D. Freeman, *Midnight and Noonday* (Norman: University of Oklahoma Press, 1984), 171, and Sumner County Press, July 30, 1874.

[78] Mrs. J.B. Rideout, *Six Years on the Border* (Philadelphia: Presbyterian Board of Publication, 1883), quoted in Donald White, *The Border Queen: A History of Early Day Caldwell, Kansas* (Wyandotte, Oklahoma: The Gregath Publishing Company, 1999), 269.

[79] *Wellington Monitor-Press*, August 24, 1921.

[80] Mrs. J.B. Rideout, *Six Years on the Border* (Philadelphia: Presbyterian Board of Publication, 1883), quoted in Donald White, *The Border Queen: A History of Early Day Caldwell, Kansas* (Wyandotte, Oklahoma: The Gregath Publishing Company, 1999), 283-284.

[81] *Ibid.*, 284-285.

[82] *Ibid.*, 279.

[83] See *Sumner County Press*, August 23 and September 3, 1874, and G.D. Freeman, *Midnight and Noonday* (Norman: University of Oklahoma Press, 1984), chapter 28.

Chapter 6 – "Chisholm Trail can no longer be used."

[84] John P. Edwards, *Historical Atlas of Sumner County, Kansas* (Philadelphia, 1883), 9.

[85] *Ibid.*, 8.

[86] Wayne Gard, *The Chisholm Trail* (Norman: University of Oklahoma Press, 1954), 211-212.

[87] David Dary, *Red Blood and Black Ink* (Lawrence: University Press of Kansas, 1998), 79.

[88] Figures are from the *First Biennial Report of the State Board of Agriculture to the Legislature of the State of Kansas for the Years 1877-1878.*

[89] William F. Zornow, *Kansas: A History of the Jayhawk State* (Norman: University of Oklahoma Press, 1957), 165.

[90] *Sumner County Press*, December 17, 1874.

[91] *Ibid.*, January 14, 1875.

[92] *Ibid.*, April 29, 1875.

[93] *Ibid.*, February 4, 1875.

[94] William G. Cutler, *History of the State of Kansas* (Chicago: A.T. Andreas, 1883), Era of Peace, Part 9, "Farm Products Tables, Part 1."

[95] *Ibid.*, Part 10, "Farm Products Tables, Part 2" and Part 12, "Farm Products Tables, Part 4."

[96] *Sumner County Press*, March 6, 1876.

[97] *Ibid.*, June 1, 1876.

[98] *Ibid.*, August 31, 1876.

[99] *Wichita Herald*, February 23, 1877.

[100] *Sumner County Press*, July 26 and November 1, 1877.

[101] *Ibid.*, November 22, 1877.

[102] *Ibid.*, December 6, 1877.

[103] *Ibid.*, January 2, 1879. See John P. Edwards, *Historical Atlas of Sumner County, Kansas* (Philadelphia, 1883), 8, for a summary of this contest.

[104] William G. Cutler, *History of the State of Kansas* (Chicago: A.T. Andreas, 1883), Era of Peace, Part 3, "Atchison, Topeka, and Santa Fe Branch Connections in Kansas."

[105] *Ibid.*, Sumner County, Part 1, "Population."

[106] A branch of the Kansas City, Lawrence, and Southern Kansas Railway, called the Sumner County Railroad, built 18.35 miles of track south of Wellington through New Haven and to the border, where cattlemen organized the town of Hunnewell to serve as a cattle shipping center. The tracks were ready for service on June 16, 1880. See William G. Cutler, *History of the State of Kansas* (Chicago: A.T. Andreas, 1883), Era of Peace, Part 5, "Kansas City,

Lawrence, and Southern Kansas." The Atchison, Topeka, and Santa Fe took control of the railroad on May 1, 1882.

Chapter 7 – "Caldwell will be the metropolis of the southwest."

[107] See Bill O'Neal, *Henry Brown: The Outlaw Marshal* (College Station, Texas: Creative Publishing Company, 1980), 88, and *Caldwell in the 1870s and 1880s: The Rowdy Years of the Border Queen* (self published, no date), 4-5.

[108] G.D. Freeman, *Midnight and Noonday* (Norman: University of Oklahoma Press, 1984), 186.

[109] See G.D. Freeman, *Midnight and Noonday* (Norman: University of Oklahoma Press, 1984), 186, footnote 3.

[110] G.D. Freeman, *Midnight and Noonday* (Norman: University of Oklahoma Press, 1984), 198.

[111] See G.D. Freeman, *Midnight and Noonday* (Norman: University of Oklahoma Press, 1984), 186, footnote 4.

[112] See the *Caldwell Post*, July 10, 1879 and *Sumner County Press*, July 17, 1879 for the two versions.

[113] G.D. Freeman, Midnight and Noonday (Norman: University of Oklahoma Press, 1984), 188.

[114] *Wellington Banner*, Wednesday, September 25, 1872.

[115] *Sumner County Press*, Thursday, September 18, 1873.

[116] City Marshal Jones along with Constable J.A. Kirk, charged with disturbing the peace, were released after appearing before Justice of the Peace James A. Dillar. (*Sumner County Press*, Thursday, November 27, 1873).

[117] *Sumner County Press*, February 19, 1874.

[118] *Ibid.*, July 29, 1875.

[119] *Ibid.*, February 10, 1876.

[120] *Ibid.*, November 18, 1875. See also *Sumner County Press*, February 3 and October 5, 1876.

[121] Sam P. Ridings, *The Chisholm Trail: A History of the World's Greatest Cattle Trail* (Guthrie, Oklahoma: Cooperative Publishing

Company, 1936), 565-566, tells the story and sources of the information.

[122] *Sumner County Press*, December 21, 1876.

[123] *Ibid.*, March 15, 1877.

[124] *Ibid.*, October 11, 1877.

[125] *Ibid.*, December 6, 1877.

[126] *Caldwell Post*, January 2, 1879. See also *Sumner County Press*, January 2, 1879.

[127] *Caldwell Post*, February 27, 1879.

[128] *Sumner County Democrat*, July 9, 1879.

[129] *Caldwell Post*, July 24, 1879.

[130] *Ibid.*, September 25, 1879. See also the September 18, 1879 issue.

[131] *Ibid.*, September 18, 1879. Jones was called both Dan and William or "Red Bill" at various times. For example, the September 25, 1879 *Post* called him Dan while the October 30 issue called him "Wm. Jones, better known as 'Red Bill.'" The U.S. Census conducted in June 1880 showed Daniel W. Jones, 34, married to Jenny, 31, with a two-month-old son. The birth announcement appeared in the April 8, 1880 issue of the *Post*.

[132] *Caldwell Post*, October 2, 1879.

[133] Nyle H. Miller and Joseph W. Snell, *Why the West was Wild* (Norman: University of Oklahoma Press, 2003), originally published, 1963, 166.

[134] *Ibid.*, 1963, 222.

[135] Wayne Gard, *The Chisholm Trail* (Norman: University of Oklahoma Press, 1954), 251.

[136] *Caldwell Post*, November 27, 1879. See also *Caldwell Post*, January 29, 1880 for a detailed description of Maj. Odem's new brick hotel. The three-story building had a billiard parlor, barber shop, and bath rooms in the basement, a dining room and offices on the first floor, a parlor, 10 single and three double rooms on the second floor, and 16 bedrooms on the third floor..

[137] Sam P. Ridings, *The Chisholm Trail* (Guthrie, Oklahoma: Co-operative Publishing Co., 1936), 490.

Chapter 8 – "Caldwell outdid Dodge City."

[138] *Caldwell Post*, June 3, 1880.
[139] *Ibid.*, April 22 and April 29, 1880.
[140] Nyle H. Miller and Joseph W. Snell, *Why the West was Wild* (Norman: University of Oklahoma Press, 2003, originally published, 1963), 248.
[141] *Ibid.*
[142] *Caldwell Post*, April 29, 1880.
[143] *Ibid.*, May 13, 1880.
[144] Robert R. Dykstra, *The Cattle Towns* (Lincoln: University of Nebraska Press, 1983, originally published, 1968), 116.
[145] *Caldwell Post*, June 10, 1880.
[146] *Ibid.*, June 24, 1880.
[147] Wayne Gard, *The Chisholm Trail* (Norman: University of Oklahoma Press, 1954), 252-253.
[148] Daniel Fitzgerald, *Ghost Towns of Kansas: A Traveler's Guide* (Lawrence: University Press of Kansas, 1988), 193-196.
[149] Wayne Gard, *The Chisholm Trail* (Norman: University of Oklahoma Press, 1954), 253.
[150] G.D. Freeman, *Midnight and Noonday* (Norman: University of Oklahoma Press, 1984), 199.
[151] Nyle H. Miller and Joseph W. Snell, *Why the West was Wild* (Norman: University of Oklahoma Press, 2003), originally published, 1963, 168.
[152] *Caldwell Commercial*, July 1, 1880.
[153] *Ibid.*
[154] *Ibid.*, July 8, 1880.
[155] *Sumner County Democrat*, July 21, 1880.
[156] *Caldwell Commercial*, August 12, 1880.

Chapter 9 – Without any visible assets

[157] *Caldwell Commercial*, July 8, 1880.

[158] Ibid., October 7, 1880.

[159] The exact date the Red Light began and its location are disputed. The April 22, 1880 issue of *Caldwell Post* said the building had been moved from Wichita to Caldwell. The dram shop license was issued in May. Richard Lane thought the saloon was located at Fifth and Arapahoe (two blocks east of Main) while Bill O'Neal believed it was at Fourth and Chisholm (one block east of Main). City records show that it was located at the northeast corner of Fifth and Chisholm. See Rod Cook's book, *George and Maggie and the Red Light Saloon*, for more details. The 1880 United States Census listed four girls, three under 21, living with Red Light owner Mag Woods. There occupation was described as "dancing." (See Miller and Snell, *Why the West was Wild*, 250).

[160] *Caldwell Commercial*, October 14, 1880.

[161] *Ibid.*

[162] *Caldwell Post*, October 14, 1880.

[163] George Spear married Lettie Rhoades, daughter of Abraham Rhoades, on November 29, 1879, according to the *Caldwell Post*, December 4, 1879. He continued running the Red Light Saloon after George Woods was killed in August 1881.

[164] *Caldwell Post*, November 4, 1880.

[165] Robert Bader Smith, *Prohibition in Kansas: A History* (Lawrence: University Press of Kansas, 1986), 60.

[166] *Ibid.*, 63-64.

[167] G.D. Freeman, *Midnight and Noonday* (Norman: University of Oklahoma Press, 1984), 187.

[168] *Sumner County Press*, March 24, 1881.

[169] *Caldwell Commercial*, June 16, 1881 and January 5, 1882. See footnote in G.D. Freeman, *Midnight and Noonday* (Norman: University of Oklahoma Press, 1884), 274.

[170] Wayne Gard, *The Chisholm Trail* (Norman: University of Oklahoma Press, 1954), 253.

[171] *Caldwell Commercial*, August 4, 1881, *Caldwell Post*, August 4, 1881.

[172] *Ibid.*, October 27 and November 3, 1881. Councilmen who opposed Hubbell were H.C. Challes, Levi Thrailkill, and L.G. Bailey. See G.D. Freeman's *Midnight and Noonday*, Chapter 41, note 6, 251-252.

[173] Rod Cook, *George and Maggie and the Red Light Saloon* (Lincoln: iUniverse, Inc., 2003), 36.

[174] *Ibid.*, August 25, 1881, *Caldwell Post*, August 25, 1881, and G.D. Freeman, *Midnight and Noonday* (Norman: University of Oklahoma Press, 1884), 203.

[175] *Sumner County Press*, December 22, 1881.

[176] Nyle H. Miller and Joseph W. Snell, *Why the West was Wild* (Norman: University of Oklahoma Press, 2003), 498.

[177] *Cowley County Courant*, December 29, 1881.

[178] T.A. McNeal, *When Kansas was Young* (Topeka, Kansas: Capper Publications, Inc., 1940), 57.

[179] *Caldwell Post*, December 1, 1881.

[180] *Ibid.*

[181] *Ibid.*

[182] *Arkansas City Traveler*, December 7, 1881.

[183] *Winfield Courier*, January 12, 1882.

[184] *Arkansas City Traveler*, January 18, 1882.

[185] *Cowley County Courant*, February 9, 1882.

[186] *Ibid.*, February 23, 1882.

[187] *Ibid.*, March 2 and March 9, 1882.

[188] *Winfield Courier*, May 11, 1882.

[189] *Caldwell Commercial*, September 28, 1882.

[190] *Ibid.*, October 12, 1882.

[191] *Ibid.*, November 30, 1882.

[192] *Ibid.*, March 22, 1883.

[193] *Ibid.*, April 5, 1883.

[194] William G. Cutler, *History of the State of Kansas* (Chicago: A.T. Andreas, 1883), Sumner County, Part 7, "Societies and Banks."

Chapter 10 – "This is the fourth murder."

[195] According to county records, Dan Jones owned property in the middle of the block south of the Red Light Saloon on Chisholm. Jones bought lots 9, 11, and 13 of block 5, which was on the east side of Chisholm in the first block south of 5th (now Central), on June 21, 1880 from Charles Stone. See Sumner County Deeds, Volume 14, page 361.

[196] *Caldwell Post* and *Sumner County Press*, December 22, 1881.

[197] *Caldwell Post*, December 22, 1881.

[198] See G.D. Freeman, *Midnight and Noonday* (Norman: University of Oklahoma Press, 1884), Chapter 42, note 12, 265-26

[199] C.W. McCampbell, "W. E. Campbell, Pioneer Kansas Livestockman," *Kansas Historical Quarterly,* August, 1948 (Vol. XVI, No. 3), pages 245 to 273. Transcription by Jodi Maranchie; HTML composition by Tod Roberts; digitized with permission of The Kansas State Historical Society.

[200] G.D. Freeman, *Midnight and Noonday* (Norman: University of Oklahoma Press, 1884), 264.

[201] The *Caldwell Post*, January 4, 1883, published Thrall's circular which described Jim Talbot (alias or possible real name James Sherman) as: "about 5 feet, 10 inches high; weighs about 170 pounds; light complection (sic); light colored mustache and whiskers; light blue or gray eyes; broad face, high cheek bones; nose turned up a little at the end; low, narrow forehead; his under jaw is the longest; when he shuts his mouth ;his teeth projects (sic) out past upper ones; generally gambles and carouses around saloons...". The paper also included detailed descriptions of Bob Bigtree, Dick Eddleman, Doug Hill, Tom Love, Jim Martin, and Bob Munson.

[202] *Wichita Eagle*, December 22, 1881 and *Wichita Beacon,* December 28, 1881.

[203] *Caldwell Commercial*, January 26, 1882.

[204] G.D. Freeman, *Midnight and Noonday* (Norman: University of Oklahoma Press, 1984), 267.

[205] Wayne Gard, *The Chisholm Trail* (Norman: University of Oklahoma Press, 1954), 254-255.

[206] *Arkansas City Traveler*, Wednesday, April 12, 1882.

[207] See footnotes in G.D. Freeman, *Midnight and Noonday* (Norman: University of Oklahoma Press, 1984), 206.

[208] *Caldwell Post*, April 20, 1882.

[209] Oliver Nelson, *The Cowman's Southwest* (Norman: University of Nebraska Press, 1986), 90-91.

[210] *Caldwell Commercial*, June 29, 1882.

[211] Nyle H. Miller and Joseph W. Snell, *Why the West was Wild* (Norman: University of Oklahoma Press, 2003), originally published, 1963, 61.

Chapter 11 – "It took a man with a great deal of nerve."

[212] *Caldwell Post*, October 26, 1882.

[213] Nyle H. Miller and Joseph W. Snell, *Why the West was Wild* (Norman: University of Oklahoma Press, 2003), originally published, 1963, 66.

[214] *Caldwell Commercial*, June 29, 1882.

[215] *Ibid.*, July 6, 1882.

[216] Charles Francis Colcord, *Autobiography of Charles Francis Colcord* (Tulsa, Oklahoma: Privately reprinted by C.C. Helmerich, 1970), 112.

[217] G.D. Freeman, *Midnight and Noonday* (Norman: University of Oklahoma Press, 1984), 212.

[218] *Ibid.*, 211.

[219] *Caldwell Post*, July 13, 1882.

[220] *Caldwell Commercial*, July 20, 1882.

[221] *Ibid.*, August 24, 1882.

[222] *Ibid.*, September 7, 1882.

[223] *Ibid.*, September 28 and October 5, 1882.

[224] *Caldwell Post*, October 12, 1882. Also, *Caldwell Commercial*, October 12, 1882.

[225] *Caldwell Commercial*, November 9, 1882.

[226] *Caldwell Post*, November 9 and November 23, 1882.

[227] Wiedeman told this to Harry Sinclair Drago. See Drago's book, *Wild, Woolly & Wicked*, page 264 and the *Caldwell Messenger*, May 8, 1961 for accounts of this claim.

[228] See G.D. Freeman's *Midnight and Noonday*, footnote 7, page 214.

Chapter 12 – "The boys would make exellent constables."

[229] Charles A. Siringo, *History of "Billy the Kid"* (Santa Fe: Charles A. Siringo, 1920), 69-70.

[230] Bill O'Neal, *Henry Brown, The Outlaw-Marshal* (College Station, Texas: Creative Publishing Co., 1980), 75.

[231] As quoted in Bill O'Neal, *Henry Brown, The Outlaw-Marshal* (College Station, Texas: Creative Publishing Co., 1980), 76.

[232] *Ibid.*, 82.

[233] See previous chapter for Charles Colcord and Andrew Drumm's role in hiring Henry Newton Brown.

[234] *Caldwell Post*, September 28, 1882 and *Caldwell Commercial*, October 12, 1882.

[235] Bill O'Neal, *Henry Brown, The Outlaw-Marshal* (College Station, Texas: Creative Publishing Co., 1980), 102.

[236] *Caldwell Post*, January 4, 1883 and *Caldwell Commercial*, January 4, 1883. The correct wording on the plate can be seen in pictures of the rifle. For example, see Joseph G. Rosa, *Guns of the American West* (New York: Exeter Books, 1988), 138.

[237] *Caldwell Commercial*, January 11, 1883.

[238] Bill O'Neal, *Henry Brown, The Outlaw-Marshal* (College Station, Texas: Creative Publishing Co., 1980), 104.

[239] Henry Nash Smith, *Virgin Land: The American West as Symbol and Myth* (New York: Vintage Press, 1957, originally published, 1950), 124-125.

[240] *Wellington Wellingtonian*, February 15 and June 28, 1883; and *Caldwell Commercial*, December 20, 1883.

[241] *Caldwell Commercial*, March 29, 1883.

[242] Robert R. Dykstra, *The Cattle Towns* (Lincoln: University of Nebraska Press, 1983, originally published, 1968), 212.

[243] *Caldwell Commercial*, April 12, 1883.

[244] Glenn Shirley, *Pawnee Bill: A Biography of Major Gordon W. Lillie* (Lincoln: University of Nebraska Press, 1965, originally published, 1958), 94. See also *Caldwell Journal*, May 17, 1883.

[245] *Caldwell Journal*, May 24, 1883.

[246] *Ibid.*, May 31, 1883.

[247] Wayne Gard, *The Chisholm Trail* (Norman: University of Oklahoma Press, 1954), 255-256.

[248] *Caldwell Journal*, May 31, 1883.

[249] Nyle H. Miller and Joseph W. Snell, *Why the West was Wild* (Norman: University of Oklahoma Press, 2003, originally published, 1963), 73.

[250] *Caldwell Journal*, August 9, 1883.

[251] Laban Samuel Records, *Cherokee Outlet Cowboy: Recollections of Laban S. Records* (Norman: University of Oklahoma Press, 1995), 191-192.

[252] *Ibid.*, 255.

[253] Oliver Nelson, *The Cowman's Southwest* (Lincoln: University of Nebraska Press, 1986), 178.

[254] Edward Everett Dale, "The Cherokee Live Stock Association," *Chronicles of Oklahoma* 5, no. 1 (March, 1927): 67-70.

[255] "It was necessary in those days to know the weight as well as the value of money, and therefore it was a matter of current knowledge that one thousand dollars in silver weighed sixty-two and one-half pounds." David Dary, *Cowboy Culture* (Lawrence: University Press of Kansas, 1981), 167.

[256] Robert Sabbag, *Too Tough to Die* (New York: Simon & Schuster, 1992), 47.

[257] *Caldwell Journal*, October 11, 1883.

[258] *Ibid.* Bill O'Neal, relying on a buckboard driver's memory from a much later time, dated the dangerous journey one year early.

See *Henry Brown, The Outlaw-Marshal* (College Station, Texas: Creative Publishing Co., 1980), 92-93.

[259] *Ibid.*, November 22, 1883.

[260] *Ibid.*, December 20, 1883.

Chapter 13 – "That they brought disgrace on the city, no one can help."

[261] *Caldwell Journal*, March 27, 1884.

[262] Bill O'Neal, *Henry Brown, The Outlaw-Marshal* (College Station, Texas: Creative Publishing Co., 1980), 120.

[263] *Caldwell Journal*, May 2, 1884.

[264] *Ibid.*, April 10, 1884; Bill O'Neal, *Henry Brown, The Outlaw-Marshal* (College Station, Texas: Creative Publishing Co., 1980), 122.

[265] *Ibid.*, May 8, 1884.

[266] Oliver Nelson, *The Cowman's Southwest*, ed. Angie Debo (Lincoln: University of Nebraska Press, 1986, originally published, 1953), 188-189. The "windbag" Nelson mentioned was probably W.C. "I Bar" Johnson, who testified after the Medicine Lodge event. (See *Medicine Lodge Cresset*, May 8, 1884). As Nelson later said, "It seems their [Brown, Wheeler, Smith, and Wesley's] confederate in the Wildcat Pool [Eagle Chief Pool] held a bunch of Indian ponies Smith and Wesley had left for him to hide, as did several other worthy citizens around Medicine. They must have figured that if the boys passed out, the ponies would stay with them. Anyhow it was this confederate that warned the bank, and the town was ready." (See Nelson, 207).

[267] Cowboy Laban Records, while working for Frank Bates at the Spade Ranch in 1880, knew Wesley as John West and said his real name was John Dugan. See Records' book, *Cherokee Outlet Cowboy* (Norman: University of Oklahoma Press, 1995), 134-135.

[268] Joe McNeal's brother, Tom, later mentioned this alleged plot in his book, *When Kansas Was Young*. See also Records' book, *Cherokee Outlet Cowboy*, 257-258.

[269] *Caldwell Journal*, May 8, 1884.

[270] Quoted in Nyle H. Miller and Joseph W. Snell, *Why the West was Wild* (Norman: University of Oklahoma Press, 2003, originally published, 1963), 77.

[271] *Caldwell Journal*, May 8, 1884.

[272] Oliver Nelson, *The Cowman's Southwest*, ed. Angie Debo (Lincoln: University of Nebraska Press, 1986, originally published, 1953), 208.

[273] *Caldwell Messenger*, December 10, December 17, and December 24, 2003.

[274] *Caldwell Journal*, October 23, 1884.

[275] *Ibid.*, November 20, 1884.

Chapter 14 – "Thus is added another victim killed by unknown parties."

[276] Oliver Nelson, *The Cowman's Southwest* (Lincoln: University of Nebraska Press, 1986, originally published, 1953), edited by Angie Debo, 218-219.

[277] Wayne Gard, *The Chisholm Trail* (Norman: University of Oklahoma Press, 1954), 259-260.

[278] Glenn Shirley, *Pawnee Bill: A Biography of Major Gordon W. Lillie* (Lincoln: University of Nebraska Press, 1965, originally published, 1958), 94-95.

[279] *Caldwell Journal*, September 3, 1885.

[280] *Ibid.*, December 10, 1885.

[281] *Sumner County Press*, December 24, 1885. The paper described Jones as "a well known figure in border troubles in Sumner County" who had been "considered something of a desperado and a 'tough man'."

[282] *Ibid.*, December 31, 1885. An anonymous Jones defender from Caldwell admitted Jones could be a little wild. "Though in early days he may have danced and drank like a great many of our young men, he never was a gambler and was always opposed to gambling and houses of ill fame in our town," the Jones defender

said. Jones himself described his past similarly, saying, "I do not
claim that my life in the west has not been a little wild, but I do not
think it has been over an average of my old associates and I do
claim that the word desperado does not apply to me." At least two
occasions of his wildness appeared in papers both early and late in
his career as a lawman. See *Sumner County Press*, November 27,
1873 and *Caldwell Post* and *Caldwell Commercial*, October 27,
1881) for these accounts. Yet he had many highly respected friends.
Among those who vouched for him were leading citizens such as
Ab Shearman, Newt Caldwell, E.C. Ferguson, George W. Haines,
I.N. Cooper, Win Corzine, I.B. Gilmore, Sim Donaldson, and John
W. Nyce.

[283] G.D. Freeman, *Midnight and Noonday* (Norman: University
of Oklahoma Press, 1984), 273.

[284] Frederick Merk, *History of the Westward Movement* (New
York: Alfred A. Knopf, 1978), 466.

[285] The markers were commissioned by the Cherokee Strip
Centennial Committee in 1992. Members of the Historic Marker
Subcommittee were Colin Wood, Richard Lowe, Harold Sturm, J.E.
Turner, Donald White, and David Williams.

Bibliography

Abbott, Edward Charles and Helena Huntington Smith. *We Pointed Them North: Recollections of a Cowpuncher.* Norman: University of Oklahoma Press, 1955 (Originally published, 1939).

Adams, Andy. *The Log of a Cowboy.* Lincoln: University of Nebraska Press, 1964 (Originally published, 1903).

Adams, Ramon F. *The Old-Time Cowhand.* Lincoln: University of Nebraska Press, 1989 (Originally published, 1948).

Alley, J. Mark. *The Violent Years: The Founding of a Kansas Town.* Hillsboro, Kansas: Prairie Books, 1992.

Bader, Robert Smith. *Prohibition in Kansas: A History.* Lawrence: University Press of Kansas, 1986.

Barnard, Edward S., ed. *Story of the Great American West.* Pleasantville, New York: The Reader's Digest Association, Inc., 1977.

Beebe, Lucius, and Charles Clegg. *U.S. West: The Saga of Wells Fargo.* New York: Bonanza Books, 1959.

Bergon, Frank, and Zeese Papanikolas, eds. *Looking Far West: The Search for the American West in History, Myth, and Literature.* New York: The New American Library, 1978.

Billington, Ray Allen. *America's Frontier Heritage.* Albuquerque: University of New Mexico Press, 1974. (Originally published, 1963).

Billington, Ray Allen. *The Westward Movement in the United States.* New York: D. Van Nostrand Co., 1959.

Billington, Ray Allen and Martin Ridge. *Westward Expansion: A History of the American Frontier,* Fifth Edition. New York: Macmillan Publishing Co., Inc., 1982.

Blackburn, Forrest R., and others, eds. *Kansas and the West: Bicentennial Essays in Honor of Nyle H. Miller.* Topeka: Kansas State Historical Society, 1976.

Blevins, Win. *Dictionary of the American West.* Seattle: Sasquatch Books, 2001.

Bogue, Allan G., Thomas D. Phillips, and James E. Wright, eds. The *West of the American People.* Itasca, Illinois: F.E. Peacock Publishers, Inc., 1970.

Boucher, Troy. *Prince of the Plains.* College Station, Texas: Virtualbookworm.com Publishing, Inc., 2002.

Brandon, William. *The American Heritage Book of Indians.* New York: Dell Publishing Co., Inc., 1973. (Originally published, 1961).

Brash, Sarah, ed. *The American Story: Settling the West.* Richmond, Virginia: Time Life, Inc., 1996.

Breihan, Carl W. *Great Lawmen of the West.* New York: Bonanza Books, 1963.

Bright, John D., ed. *Kansas: The First Century.* Volume I thru IV. New York: Lewis Historical Publishing Company, 1956.

Brown, Dee. *The American West.* New York: Simon & Schuster, 1994.

Brown, Dee, with Martin F. Schmitt. *Trail Driving Days.* New York: Charles Scribner's Sons, 1952.

Bryant, Keith L. *History of the Atchison, Topeka and Santa Fe Railway.* Lincoln: University of Nebraska Press, 1982. (Originally published, 1974).

Burton, Art T. *Black, Red and Deadly: Black and Indian Gunfighters of the Indian Territories, 1870-1907.* Austin, Texas: Eakin Press, 1991.

Calhoun, Frederick S. *The Lawmen: United States Marshals and their Deputies, 1789-1989.* Washington, D.C.: Smithsonian Institution Press, 1989.

Castel, Albert. *A Frontier State at War: Kansas, 1861-1865.* Ithaca, New York: American Historical Association, Cornell University Press, 1958.

Chrisman, Harry E. *1001 Most-Asked Questions About the American West.* Athens, Ohio: Swallow Press Books, Ohio University Press, 1982.

Coke, Tom S. *Old West Justice in Belle Plaine, Kansas.* Bowie, Maryland: Heritage Books, Inc., 2002.

Colbert, David, ed. *Eyewitness to the American West: From the Aztec Empire to the Digital Frontier in the Words of Those Who Saw It Happen.* New York: Viking Press, 1998.

Colcord, Charles Francis. *Autobiography of Charles Francis Colcord.* Tulsa, Oklahoma: Privately reprinted by C.C. Helmerich, 1970.

Cook, Rod. *George and Maggie and the Red Light Saloon: Depravation, Debauchery, Violence, and Sundry Cussedness in a Kansas Cowtown.* Lincoln, Nebraska: iUniverse, Inc., 2003.

Cox, James. *Historical and Biographical Record of the Cattle Industry and the Cattlemen of Texas and Adjacent Territory* (Two Volumes). New York: Antiquarian Press, Ltd., 1959.

Dary, David. *The Buffalo Book: The Saga of an American Symbol.* New York: Avon Books, 1974.

Dary, David. *Cowboy Culture: A Saga of Five Centuries.* Lawrence: University of Kansas Press, 1989. (Originally published, 1981).

Drago, Harry Sinclair. *Wild, Wooly & Wicked: The History of the Kansas Cow Towns And the Texas Cattle Trade.* New York: Clarkson N. Potter, Inc., 1960.

_____. *Road Agents and Train Robbers: Half a Century of Western Banditry.* New York: Dodd, Mead & Co., 1973.

Dykstra, Robert R. *The Cattle Towns.* Lincoln: University of Nebraska Press, 1968, 1983.

Einsel, Mary. *Stagecoach West to Kansas: True Stories of the Kansas Plains.* Boulder, Colorado: Pruett Publishing Company, 1970.

Erdoes, Richard R. *Saloons of the Old West.* Avenel, New Jersey: Gramercy Books, 1997. (Originally published, 1979).

Etulain, Richard W. & Glenda Riley, eds. *With Badges and Bullets: Lawmen & Outlaws in the Old West.* Golden, Colorado: Fulcrum Publishing, 1999.

Federal Writer's Project of the Work Projects Administration for the State of Kansas. *The WPA Guide to 1930's Kansas.* Lawrence: University Press of Kansas, 1984. (Originally published, 1939).

Federal Writer's Project of the Work Projects Administration for the State of Oklahoma. *The WPA Guide to 1930's Oklahoma.* Lawrence: University Press of Kansas, 1986. (Originally published, 1941).

Fitzgerald, Daniel. *Ghost Towns of Kansas: A Traveler's Guide.* Lawrence: University Press of Kansas, 1988.

_____. *Faded Dreams: More Ghost Towns of Kansas.* Lawrence: University Press of Kansas, 1994.

Flaherty, Thomas H., ed. *The Wild West.* New York: Time Warner Co., 1993.

Flanagan, Mike. *The Complete Idiot's Guide to The Old West.* New York: Alpha Books, 1999.

Forbis, William H. *The Cowboys.* New York: Time-Life Books, Inc., 1973.

Fradkin, Philip L. *Stagecoach: Wells Fargo and the American West.* New York: Free Press, 2002.

Frazier, Ian. *Great Plains.* New York: Farrar / Straus / Giroux, 1989.

Freeman, G.D. *Midnight and Noonday or the Incidental History of Southern Kansas and the Indian Territory, 1871-1890.* Norman: University of Oklahoma Press, 1984 Edited with an Introduction and Notes, by Richard L. Lane. (Originally published, 1890).

Gard, Wayne. *The Chisholm Trail.* Norman: University of Oklahoma Press, 1954.

_____. *Frontier Justice.* Norman: University of Oklahoma Press, 1949.

_____. *The Great Buffalo Hunt: Its history and drama, and its role in the opening of the West.* Lincoln: University of Nebraska Press, 1959.

Hardin, John Wesley. *The Life of John Wesley Hardin as Written by Himself.* Norman: University of Oklahoma Press, 1961. (Originally published, 1896).

Harman, Samuel W. *Hell on the Border.* Lincoln: University of Nebraska Press, 1992 (Originally published, 1898).

Hine, Robert V. *The American West: An Interpretive History.* Boston: Little, Brown and Company, 1973.

Horan, James D. *The Gunfighters: The Authentic Wild West.* New York: Gramercy Books, 1994. (Originally published, 1976).

_____. *The Lawmen: The Authentic Wild West.* New York: Gramercy Books, 1996. (Originally published, 1980).

_____. *The Outlaws: The Authentic Wild West.* New York: Gramercy Books, Books, 1995. (Originally published, 1977).

Hough, Emerson. *The Passing of the Frontier: A Chronicle of the Old West.* New Haven: Yale University Press, 1918.

Ise, John. *Sod and Stubble: The Story of a Kansas Homestead.* Lincoln: University of Nebraska Press, 1967. (Originally published, 1936).

Kansas Atlas & Gazetteer: Topographic Maps of the Entire State, First Edition. Yarmouth, Maine: DeLorme, 1997.

Lake, Stuart N. *Wyatt Earp: Frontier Marshal.* Boston: Houghton Mifflin, 1931.

Lamar, Howard Roberts, ed. *The New Encyclopedia of the American West.* New Haven & London: Yale University Press, 1977. (Originally published, 1977).

Lewis, Jon E. *The Mammoth Book of the West.* New York: Carroll & Graf Publishers, Inc., 1996.

Locke, Raymond Friday, ed. *The American West.* Los Angeles: Mankind Publishing Company, 1971.

Long, R. M. "Dick". *Wichita Century: A Pictorial History of Wichita, Kansas, 1870-1970.* Wichita: The Wichita Historical Museum Association, Inc., 1969.

Longstreet, Stephen. *War Cries On Horseback: The Story of the Indian Wars of the Great Plains.* Garden City, New York: Doubleday & Company, Inc., 1970.

McCoy, Joseph G. *Historic Sketches of the Cattle Trade of the West and Southwest.* Kansas City: Ramsey, Millett & Hudson, 1874.

McLoughlin, Denis. *Wild and Woolly: An Encyclopedia of the Old West.* New York: Barnes & Noble, Inc., 1996. (Originally published, 1975).

McNeal, T.A. *When Kansas Was Young.* New York: Macmillan Company, 1922.

Merk, Frederick. *History of the Westward Movement.* New York: Alfred A. Knopf, Inc., 1978.

Metz, Leon Claire. *The Encyclopedia of Lawmen, Outlaws, and Gunfighters.* New York: Facts on File, 2003.

_____. *The Shooters.* New York: Berkley Books, 1996. (Originally published, 1976).

Miller, Benjamin S. *Ranching in Southwest Kansas and Indian Territory.* New York: Fless & Ridge Co., 1896.

Miller, Nyle H., and Joseph W. Snell. *Great Gunfighters of the Kansas Cowtowns, 1867-1886.* Lincoln: University of Nebraska Press, 1963.

_____. *Why the West was Wild: A Contemporary Look at the Antics of Some Highly Publicized Kansas Cowtown Personalities.* Topeka: Kansas State Historical Society, 1963.

Milner, Clyde A., Carol A. O'Connor, and others, eds. *The Oxford History of the American West.* New York: Oxford University Press, 1994.

Miner, Craig. *Kansas: The History of the Sunflower State, 1854-2000.* Lawrence: University Press of Kansas, 2002.

_____. *West of Wichita: Settling the High Plains of Kansas, 1865-1890.* Lawrence: University Press of Kansas, 1986.

_____. *Wichita: The Early Years, 1865-1880.* Lincoln: University of Nebraska Press, 1989.

_____. *Wichita: The Magic City: An Illustrated History.* Wichita, Kansas: Wichita-Sedgwick County Historical Museum Association, 1989.

Monaghan, Jay, (ed.). *The Book of the American West.* New York: Bonanza Books, 1963.

Morgan, Ted. *A Shovel of Stars: The Making of the American West – 1800 to the Present.* New York: Simon and Schuster, 1995.

Morris, John W., Charles R. Goins, and Edwin C. McReynolds. *Historical Atlas of Oklahoma,* Third Edition. Norman: University of Oklahoma Press, 1986.

Myers, John Myers. *Bravos of the West.* Lincoln: University of Nebraska Press, 1962, 1990.

Nash, Jay Robert. *Encyclopedia of Western Lawmen and Outlaws.* New York: De Capo Press, 1994.

Nelson, Oliver. *Cowman's Southwest: Being the Reminiscences of Oliver Nelson, freighter, camp cook, cowboy, frontiersman in Kansas, Indian Territory, Texas, and Oklahoma, 1878-1893.* Edited by Angie Debo. Lincoln: University of Nebraska Press, 1986. (Originally published, 1953).

Nix, Evett Dumas, as told to Gordon Hines. *Oklahombres: Particularly the Wilder Ones.* Lincoln: University of Nebraska Press, 1993. (Originally published, 1929).

Oklahoma Atlas & Gazetteer: Topographic Maps of the Entire State, First Edition. Yarmouth, Maine: DeLorme, 1998.

O'Neal, Bill. *Caldwell in the 1870's and 1880's: The Rowdy Years of the Border Queen.* Privately published, date unknown.

_____. *Encyclopedia of Western Gunfighters.* Norman: University of Oklahoma Press, 1979.

_____. *Henry Brown: The Outlaw-Marshall.* College Station, Texas: Creative Publishing Company, Early West Series, 1980.

Phillips, Charles. *Heritage of the West.* New York: Crescent Books, 1992.

Polley, Jane, ed. *American Folklore and Legend.* Pleasantville, N.Y.: Reader's Digest Association, 1978.

Prassel, Frank Richard. *The Western Peace Officer: A Legacy of Law and Order.* Norman: University of Oklahoma Press, 1972.

Preston, Ralph & Monte. *Early Kansas: An Historical Atlas.* Tidewater, Oregon: Pioneer Press, 1997.

Rabinowitz, Harold Preston. *Black Hats and White Hats: Heroes and Villains of the West.* New York: Metro Books, 1996.

Records, Laban Samuel. *Cherokee Outlet Cowboy.* Ed., Ellen Jayne Maris Wheeler. University of Oklahoma Press, 1995.

Richmond, Robert W. *Kansas: A Land of Contrasts.* St. Louis, Missouri: Forum Press, 1980. (Originally published, 1974).

Richmond, Robert W., and Robert W. Mardock, eds. *A Nation Moving West: Readings in the History of the American Frontier.* Lincoln: University of Nebraska Press, 1966.

Rideout, Mrs. J.B. *Six Years on the Border; or, Sketches of Frontier Life.* Philadelphia: Presbyterian Board of Publication, 1883.

Ridings, Sam P. *The Chisholm Trail.* Guthrie, Oklahoma: Co-operative Publishing Co., 1936.

Rosa, Joseph G. *Age of the Gunfighter: Men and Weapons on the Frontier 1840-1900.* Norman: University of Oklahoma Press, 1995.

_____. *The Gunfighter: Man or Myth?* Norman: University of Oklahoma Press, 1969.

_____. *They Called Him Wild Bill: The Life and Adventures of James Butler Hickok.* Norman: University of Oklahoma Press, 1964.

Ruede, Howard, Edited by John Ise. *Sod-House Day: Letters from a Kansas Homesteader, 1877-78.* Lawrence: University Press of Kansas, 1983. (Originally published, 1937).

Russell, Don. *The Lives and Legends of Buffalo Bill.* Norman: University of Oklahoma Press, 1960.

Sabbag, Robert. *Too Tough to Die: Down and Dangerous with the U.S. Marshals.* New York: Simon & Schuster, 1992.

Sandoz, Mari. *The Cattlemen.* Lincoln: University of Nebraska Press, 1978.

Savage, William W., Jr. *The Cherokee Strip Live Stock Association: Federal Regulation and the Cattleman's Last Frontier.* Norman: University of Oklahoma Press, 1973.

Schmitt, Martin F., with Dee Brown. *The Settlers' West.* New York: Ballantine Books, 1974 (Originally published, 1955).

Shirley, Glenn. *Bell Starr and Her Times: The Literature, the Facts, and the Legends.* Norman: University of Oklahoma Press, 1990.

———. *Law West of Fort Smith.* Lincoln: University of Nebraska Press, 1957, 1986.

———. *Pawnee Bill: A Biography of Major Gordon W. Lillie.* Lincoln: University of Nebraska Press, 1958.

Siringo, Charles A. *A Texas Cowboy.* Lincoln: University of Nebraska Press, 1950, 1979. (Originally published, 1886).

Smith, Henry Nash. *Virgin Land: The American West as Symbol and Myth.* New York: Vintage Books, 1959.

Smith, Robert Barr. *Daltons!* Norman: University of Oklahoma Press, 1996.

Sutherland, Daniel E. *The Expansion of Everyday Life: 1860-1876.* New York: Harper & Row Publishers, 1989.

Taylor, Dick. "Tom 'Bear River' Smith," *Kansas Collection Articles* date unknown.

Tefertiller, Casey. *Wyatt Earp: The Life Behind the Legend.* New York: John Wiley & Sons, Inc., 1997.

Texas Atlas & Gazetteer: Detailed Topographic Maps, Fourth Edition. Yarmouth, Maine: DeLorme, 2001.

Trachtman, Paul. *The Gunfighters.* Alexandria, Virginia: Time-Life Books, Inc., 1974.

Turner, Frederick Jackson. *Frontier and Section.* Englewood Cliffs, New Jersey: Prentice-Hall, Inc., 1961.

Utley, Robert. *Billy the Kid: A Short and Violent Life.* Lincoln: University of Nebraska Press, 1989.

———. *Frontier Regulars: The United States Army and the Indian, 1866-1891.* Lincoln: University of Nebraska Press, 1973.

Vestal, Stanley. *Dodge City: Queen of Cowtowns.* Lincoln: University of Nebraska Press, 1998. (Originally published, 1952).

Webb, Walter Prescott. *The Great Plains.* New York: Grosset & Dunlap, 1931, 1971.

_____. *The Texas Rangers: A Century of Frontier Defense.* Austin: University of Texas Press, 1995 (Originally published, 1935).

Wellman, Paul I. *A Dynasty of Western Outlaws.* New York: Doubleday, 1961.

_____. *The Trampling Herd: The Story of the Cattle Range in America.* Garden City, New York: Doubleday & Company, Inc., 1961. (Originally published 1939).

White, Richard. *"It's Your Misfortune and None of My Own": A New History of the American West.* Norman: University of Oklahoma Press, 1991.

Wood, L. Curtise. *Dynamics of Faith: Wichita 1870-1897.* Wichita, Kansas: Wichita State University, 1969.

Writer's Program of the Work Projects Administration in the State of Oklahoma. *The WPA Guide to 1930's Oklahoma.* Lawrence: University Press of Kansas, 1986. (Originally published, 1941).

Yost, Nellie Snyder. *Medicine Lodge: The Story of a Kansas frontier town.* Chicago: The Swallow Press, Inc., 1970.

Young, Fredric R. *Dodge City: Up Through a Century in Story and Pictures.* Dodge City: Boot Hill Museum, Inc., 1972.

Zornow, William Frank. *Kansas: A History of the Jayhawk State.* Norman: University of Oklahoma Press, 1957.

Index

ABOUT THE AUTHOR

Tom S. Coke, born and raised in Wichita, Kansas, became interested in the Old West at an early age. A graduate of Wichita State University (B.A.) and a theological seminary near Chicago (M.A.), he now works as a freelance writer. He has written articles for a number of periodicals, including *Wild West* magazine. His book, *Old West Justice in Belle Plaine, Kansas* (Heritage Books, Inc.), was published in 2002. He and his wife now live south of Wichita surrounded by horses, dogs, cats, chickens, ducks, and a goat.

1041469

Made in the USA